PRAISE FOR THE AUTHOR

"Danny and his team bring a high level of insight, knowledge, and integrity to the online business world."

-GUY KAWASAKI, CHIEF EVANGELIST OF CANVA
AND AUTHOR OF *THE ART OF THE START 2.0*

"I've been consistently impressed with Danny; not just how smart he is, but also how giving he is with his expertise and generous spirit."

-BRIAN KURTZ, FOUNDER OF TITANS MARKETING LLC
AND AUTHOR OF *OVERDELIVER*

"Danny and his team are a model of professionalism and quality. Anyone who's serious about online marketing should be following what they're doing."

-MICHAEL PORT, *NEW YORK TIMES* BEST-SELLING AUTHOR
OF *STEAL THE SHOW*

"Danny Iny and his organization are an utterly thorough and high-quality team of people delivering excellent products. I love sending people to Danny and team because I know they're in good hands and will come out the other end super smart and ready to tackle the world."

-CHRIS BROGAN, CEO OWNER MEDIA GROUP

"He's always full of energy, insight, and passion for what people need to learn to truly be successful. I would not hesitate to recommend him or his company, based solely on his kindness, integrity, and intensity."

-MITCH JOEL, AUTHOR OF *SIX PIXELS OF SEPARATION* AND *CTRL ALT DELETE*

"Danny Iny always provides solid content you can apply to grow your business. He's the real deal."

-RANDY GAGE, AUTHOR OF THE *NEW YORK TIMES* BESTSELLER *RISKY IS THE NEW SAFE*

"Danny Iny is revolutionizing internet marketing, courses, and all other forms of online education. His enlightened approach to generating a sustainable model for ongoing income and impact is rivaled only by the level of integrity that is present in everything that he does."

-HAL ELROD, AUTHOR OF *THE MIRACLE MORNING*

"Danny Iny is a superhero, plain and simple. It's why I endorse his products to my people, without hesitation. His only burning desire is to help his sphere of influence build long-term online business that changes lives and create freedom."

-ANDRE CHAPERON, CREATOR OF AUTORESPONDER MADNESS

"Danny and his team have built something truly special in the online business world: a place that people can go to learn, grow, and work in partnership with a company that cares as much about their success as they do."
-CLAY COLLINS, CO-FOUNDER OF LEADPAGES AND NOMICS

"Danny Iny is one of the smartest minds in the online marketing space. The work he and the entire Mirasee team are doing is truly industry leading. Above all else, they genuinely care about delivering results for their clients and students, which is far too rare these days!"
-JOSH TURNER, FOUNDER OF LINKEDSELLING
AND AUTHOR OF *BOOKED*

"When it comes to building your audience and designing online courses, Danny Iny is one of few experts I trust and personally follow – and someone I recommend all my customers follow as well."
-RYAN LEVESQUE, AUTHOR OF *ASK* AND *CHOOSE*

"Danny is one of the very few that care about his customers, stay ahead of the crowd, and produce results for himself, his clients, and his customers."
-RYAN MORAN, FOUNDER OF CAPITALISM.COM

"We've all heard the old adage about "teaching a man to fish." I love Danny's ethic because he doesn't believe in doing things any other way. A fantastic teacher, a brilliant entrepreneur, and exactly the type of guy I'd love to have on my team (if I couldn't have him leading it)."
-SEAN PLATT, FOUNDER AND CEO STERLING & STONE

TEACH
your
Gift

**How Coaches, Consultants,
Authors, Speakers and Experts
Create Online Course Business
Success in 2020 and Beyond**

Danny Iny

MIRASEE PRESS

5750 Avenue Notre Dame de Grace
Montreal, Quebec
H4A 1M4, Canada
www.mirasee.com

Paperback ISBN: 978-1-7347725-1-7
Hardback ISBN: 978-1-7347725-0-0
E-book ISBN: 978-1-7347725-2-4

1 3 5 7 9 10 8 6 4 2

This book is dedicated to my students; every day, I'm awed by your expertise, inspired by your humility and grit, and energized by your dedication to make the world a little bit better by teaching your gifts.

DOWNLOAD THE AUDIOBOOK + COURSE BUSINESS TOOL KIT (FOR FREE)!

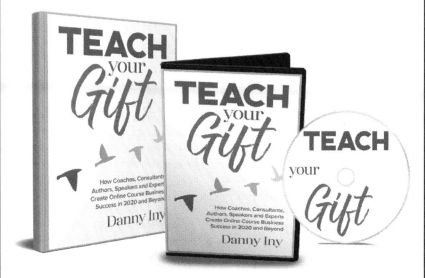

READ THIS FIRST

Just to say thank you for reading my book, I'd love to share the audiobook version PLUS our accompanying Course Business Tool Kit, at no cost whatsoever—it's my gift to you. — *Danny Iny*

Go to **TeachYour.Gift/toolkit** to get it!

CONTENTS

HOW ONLINE COURSES CHANGED MY LIFE (TWICE!)

"The second we embrace change, we become
open to the limitless possibilities of life."
-MICHELLE MAROS

MY HEART POUNDED and my fingers trembled as my eyes darted across my online banking statement. My accounts were all empty, and my credit cards were maxed out. I felt shell-shocked. My start-up company had crumbled, and my last employee was gone. What was I going to do? Circumstances had left me with over a quarter of a million dollars of debt, and my consulting practice had completely dried up. I had no money, no income, and no prospects... only debt. How did I get here?

I wanted to make the world a better place, and I thought I'd do it with a start-up company. We built educational software to help kids learn how to read. I bootstrapped the company through prototypes, proof of concept, a product launch, and market testing. The product was great—kids loved it, and so did the experts in the field.

But I was young and inexperienced, and I made a mistake. Parents and teachers—our actual customers—didn't get it. We were bleeding money but managed to pivot the product to an educational virtual world for kids. Feedback was spectacular, and all we needed was money to make it happen. I spent every penny I had to keep it going long enough for an investor to write us a check, and just as we were getting tantalizingly close... the market crash of 2008 hit. Game over. I was so far in the red that I forgot there were other colors. I had to let my employees go, and wind down the company. Meanwhile, I had been so busy with my start-up that my consulting business had been neglected, and the pipeline was dry.

I did what anyone would do when left with no alternative: I started over. I parlayed my hard- and expensive-won expertise into a new consulting business and hit the networking circuit. I took every meeting and pursued every opportunity. And by the time a few years had passed, I was doing all right. Sure, some months were more comfortable than others, but the pain of failure was no longer so acute. I was fine.

Except that I wasn't fine. Sure, I was earning decent money, but I was also carrying so much debt that I expected to spend most of my adult life paying it off. And I wasn't exactly in love with every client I had to chase (or with the actual chasing!). But it wasn't just about money or lifestyle. I had the same nagging feeling that afflicts so many of the coaches, consultants, authors, and speakers I've met over the last decade: the feeling that I could be making more of an impact than I was. That the skills, expertise, and insights I'd spent a lifetime developing could help more than the people I happened to meet at local networking mixers.

So I started writing. I was inspired by the emerging zeitgeist of blogging and social media, and the promise that through the internet one might touch the lives of millions. I poured my heart (and my best ideas) onto the proverbial page, and agonized to make every word perfect. There was just one problem: Nobody actually read any of it. I discovered what every burgeoning online entrepreneur learns sooner or later: that creating something great is only a small piece of the puzzle of building an actual business.

I tried to learn what was missing; I read every article and book that I could get my hands on. Much of it was out of date, and even the best stuff was able to help me understand only *what* to do, not *how* to do it. I looked for experts who might be able to help, but few people seemed to have the skills I really needed, and those who did were far beyond my budget and risk tolerance. I felt stuck and stymied. Thankfully, things were about to look up.

In all my internet browsing, I stumbled across an online course being offered by a blogger, who has since become a trusted friend. He had the exact expertise I needed, and while I couldn't afford to hire him as a personal advisor, I could spring for his online course. And thank goodness that I did, because that's the first time that online courses changed my life. By applying his ideas, and then building on them with my own, I was finally able to get eyes on my work, and word began to spread. I was even starting to attract consulting clients through the internet—something that had never happened before.

Then something surprising happened. All those people who followed my work and watched my slow climb to become a D-level internet celebrity started reaching out to me with questions and requests. They wanted me to do more than just write articles—they wanted me to create an online course of my own, teaching some of the strategies that I had developed. It took some time for me to warm up to the idea, but eventually I gave it a shot. That was the second time that online courses changed my life. My small team and I were blown away by the demand; that single online course led to another, and then another. My business grew: in just a few years we went from a one-person consultancy to a team of several dozen people, serving thousands of students in our courses and coaching programs.

I feel lucky to have discovered the world of online courses early, before it was cool. But these days, the cat is clearly out of the bag.

ONLINE COURSES ARE TAKING THE WORLD BY STORM

Online courses have come a long way from their obscurity just a few years ago. Today everyone is getting in on the action—from pop stars to celebrity chefs, from relationship experts to business gurus, from athletes to authors, and everyone in between. You can get their courses from publishers like MasterClass and CreativeLive, through marketplaces like Udemy and LinkedIn Learning, and of course on the websites of hundreds of thousands of independent course creators who avail themselves of self-serve platforms like Thinkific, Teachable, and Ruzuku—all driving the rapid growth of an industry already valued at multiple hundreds of billions of dollars, as reported by TJ McCue on Forbes.

In fact, online courses have become so ubiquitous that it's easy to forget how new of a phenomenon they really are. Even a few years ago, to receive instruction from the leading experts in your field was a fantasy—unless you could afford astronomical consulting rates, or were one of the privileged few that luck or circumstance had placed in direct contact with them. But the emergence and evolution of a host of technologies has made possible the holy grail for people seeking to create impact by (and profit from) sharing their expertise: leverage.

Of course, leverage isn't a new idea. It was in the third century BCE that the Greek mathematician Archimedes famously said that with a lever long enough and a fulcrum on which to place it, he could move the world. It's a powerful idea, fundamentally about being smart with the resources that you have in order to get the most bang for your buck. That's what engineers do with physical levers and fulcrums, but it's also the concept that real estate developers use to buy much more land than the cash in their pockets is worth and that political operatives use when they trade favors in pursuit of their agendas. In all cases, they place their resources (a physical lever, the cash and credibility they've earned, or a juicy piece of gossip) where they'll get the most bang for their buck (a fulcrum, a lending institution, or a gossip columnist).

Experts aren't new to the application of leverage either, but for most of human history we were limited by the technology of the day. Yes, you know what I'm talking about—you're holding it in your hand right now. For most of human history, the primary vehicle of knowledge transfer was the book. And books are great for a lot of things; as a reader, I'm grateful to the countless authors who've opened my mind, expanded my horizons, and planted seeds in my imagination. And as a writer, I'm (grudgingly) appreciative of how the writing process forces us to refine and clarify our thinking.

But while books are great for transmitting ideas, sharing perspectives, and adding new knowledge to existing expertise, they're not very good at imparting competence or capability. Put simply, people don't usually develop skills or get good at doing things by reading about them—that takes a more involved intervention, which includes the interactivity and dynamism of meaningful and timely feedback. The way to do that for most of history has been to work closely with a teacher; whether through lectures and assignments, explicit apprenticeships, or the implicit pact between employer and employee to "learn on the job," you had to be in fairly close contact with your instructor.

But gradually over the past couple of decades, technology made possible an ever-richer learning experience that could deliver real competence and transformation to the dedicated student. And that was the gateway to real leverage.

All of a sudden, experts could meaningfully impart the transformation that their skills provide to as many students who wanted to learn and benefit. The sky was the limit, as evidenced by the throngs of learners who rushed to embrace the opportunities that they heretofore couldn't afford or access. And that excitement was music to the ears of all those intrepid course creators, who could suddenly reach far more people (and earn far more income). And it's not just about the reach or income either—the best part of it all for course entrepreneurs is the freedom:

FINANCIAL FREEDOM, FOR ONE. This isn't the only thing, but it's definitely important. Leverage means that you're no longer constrained by the direct trade of hours for dollars. I'm certainly grateful to earn a comfortable living and to have been able to pay my debts. This potential for financial return is what attracts many course creators to this opportunity.

THE FREEDOM TO CHOOSE YOUR OWN HOURS. Since you aren't directly beholden to any individual student, you don't have a clock to punch, so you can choose both how much to work and what schedule best suits you, your family, and your priorities.

THE FREEDOM TO TRAVEL. This can mean taking dream vacations, going on extended trips, spending months at a time in new destinations, or living the life of a digital nomad since just about everything that course businesses involve can be done from anywhere with a stable internet connection, and entrepreneurs aren't beholden to employers who count vacation days. **THE FREEDOM NOT TO TRAVEL.** Whereas many course entrepreneurs are excited to travel more, there are also a lot of frequent fliers who are tired of getting on planes that take them away from their lives and families on a weekly basis. The ability to serve through an online course can change business travel from a necessity to a choice. **THE FREEDOM TO DO STUFF THAT MATTERS.** This is the most important freedom of all, whether it means spending more time with your kids, scaling the impact of your expertise, or dedicating your energies to the causes that you care about.

No wonder so many experts are flocking to join the online course revolution, drawn to this alluring cocktail of leverage, freedom, and impact. I know, because I've had the privilege of being in the eye of the online courses tornado for most of the last decade. Since I got involved in this world, I've written about online courses for major publications, spoken about them at conferences and to organizations, and published multiple books as the landscape has evolved. And while I take an academic sort of interest in understanding what makes the world of online courses tick, I've also had the practical experience of working with thousands of online course creators that were trained through my company's online training programs (yes, courses about courses... it's very meta, I know!).

Over the years, I've encountered thousands of consultants, coaches, speakers, authors, and experts who are excited by the idea of what an online course can do for their businesses and lives, but aren't quite clear on what it will take to go from a good idea to a thriving course business. Or worse, they think they know, but they're working off of a playbook that's woefully out of date. Remember, we're talking about internet years here, and things have changed a lot recently! To set the record straight, and give a working blueprint that can be followed by those experts (of which I assume you are one), I wrote this book—may it support you on your journey to teach your gift.

WHAT LIES AHEAD

My goal in this book is to show you the blueprint for online course business success that works today and into the future—one that you can use to create the leverage, freedom, and impact that you know courses can add to your business and life. We'll do this through five chapters:

1. A BRIEF HISTORY OF ONLINE COURSES. We'll start with a quick review of the history of online courses. You'll learn how things came to be the way they are today, and understand the nuances of the landscape from which you'll launch your online course business.

2. YOUR COURSE AND YOUR BUSINESS. Next we'll talk about the different ways that an online course can fit into a business, and you'll decide which configuration makes the most sense for you and for your students. Getting this right is the real key to the leverage, freedom, and impact that attracts people to the world of online courses in the first place.

3. FROM GOOD IDEA TO WINNING COURSE. Here you'll learn the actual course creation blueprint: what to do first, second, and third as you turn your idea into a course, and what potholes to avoid along the way. Here I'll share some of the most powerful techniques that we teach students in our online course creation training programs.

4. HOW TO ATTRACT PAYING STUDENTS. These are the sixty-four-million-dollar questions on every course builder's mind: Where do I find paying students, and how do I enroll them in my courses? The answers will vary based on the stage of the course business journey that you're on, and we'll explore the best answer for you so that you can get the results that you're looking for.

5. CREATING A WORLD-CLASS COURSE. Finally, we'll do a deep dive into what's on the cutting edge of online course creation today so that you can both stay current and get ahead of the competition to create a course that delivers transformation and engenders testimonials, referrals, and repeat business from your students.

I've done my very best to pour my expertise into the pages (or screen) that you're holding, and I know that if you carefully read the pages ahead, you'll be dramatically better prepared to build your own thriving course business.

P.S. You do NOT need to read this entire book before also taking some next steps to connect with me and with my company Mirasee's course building and marketing training. Feel free to take advantage of the invitations on the next page NOW.

ADDITIONAL RESOURCES TO SUPPORT YOU!

GET THE AUDIOBOOK + COURSE BUSINESS TOOL KIT

Receive the free audiobook PLUS our Course Business Tool Kit, which contains valuable downloads and worksheets to help you create your own online course business.

→ Download it at **TeachYour.Gift/toolkit**

PARTICIPATE IN THE COURSE BUILDER'S BOOTCAMP

Ready to start your own online course business journey? Our weeklong intensive Course Builder's Bootcamp is a crash course in everything you need to get started.

→ Sign up for free at **TeachYour.Gift/bootcamp**

JOIN US IN PERSON AT TEACH YOUR GIFT LIVE

Receive best-in-class training, discover cutting-edge strategies, and connect with a community of your fellow coach, consultant, author, speaker, and expert course entrepreneurs.

→ Reserve your spot at **TeachYour.Gift/live**

Chapter 1

A BRIEF HISTORY OF ONLINE COURSES

*"You can't really know where you're going
until you know where you've been."*

-MAYA ANGELOU

THE FIRST EPISODE of Sarah Koenig's investigative journalism podcast *Serial* was released on October 3, 2014. It investigated the 1999 murder of Baltimore high school student Hae Min Lin, and it struck a chord—the show's episodes have been downloaded hundreds of millions of times, and prompted an explosion of the podcasting medium. Today the landscape of podcasting is booming, with every celebrity seeming to have their own show, and high-value productions coming out of studios like Pushkin Industries, Transmitter Media, and Gimlet, the latter of which was acquired in 2019 by Spotify for something in the range of $230 million. In just a few years, podcasts had exploded, seemingly out of nowhere.

Except that it wasn't out of nowhere. Podcasting has existed for longer than the term *podcasting*, starting with audioblogging that dates back to the 1980s. It existed on the fringes for decades; where hardly anybody knew it existed. It wasn't until after the 2001 advent of the iPod that distribution for those audioblogs became remotely accessible, and they came to actually be called *podcasts*. The landscape slowly evolved for another decade before there was enough kindling for the spark of *Serial* to set the industry on fire.

This process of starting on the fringes and then slowly making it into the mainstream is described in detail in Everett Rogers's 1962 book *Diffusion of Innovations*. Rogers, a professor of communication studies at the University of New Mexico, described the process through which new ideas and technologies spread through society. You may not have heard of Rogers or his theory, but you're probably familiar with the idea; if you've ever seen a bell curve divided into groups labeled "Innovators,""Early Adopters,""Early Majority," and so forth, that's where it comes from.

All innovations make their way from innovators (like the audiobloggers of the 80s) to early adopters (the podcasters of the mid-2000s) to the early majority (the modern explosion of podcasting) and so on, with predictable steps and stumbles along the way—for example, the psychology and priorities of innovators vs. early adopters vs. the early majority, and the "chasm" that these conditions create, that challenge companies (and industries) seeking to transition from early adopters to the mainstream. This is true regardless of whether the innovation in question is podcasting, the music of the Beatles, or online courses. At the same time, some things are unique to each market and opportunity. In this chapter, we'll explore what this evolution has looked like in the world of online courses, and what it means for aspiring course entrepreneurs in 2020 and beyond.

THE INNOVATOR'S GOLD RUSH (2000–2014)

Our story begins at the start of the millennium (just to put things in context, Google was founded in 1998), and back then it wasn't about courses at all; it was just about publishing content. Many of the very early successes were the result of serendipitous accident; someone with a bit of technical skill built a website on a topic that they found interesting, and one day they'd realize that their passion project was being viewed by hundreds of thousands of people. Remember, these were the early days; if you built a good website on a topic, it was probably the only one, so getting noticed was just a matter of time. Many of these early successes never set out to do more than write about something that interested them; amassing an audience was a happy accident.

But in 2003, Google changed the game by launching its AdSense platform, which allowed publishers to place a snippet of code on their sites, have ads served up to their readers, and participate in the profit that Google earned from advertisers. That's how some of the very first fortunes were made in the world of online publishing, allowing people to supplement their income, and in some cases quit their day jobs. They encouraged their friends to jump on this exciting new opportunity, and some did; thus, the circle of these online publishing businesses grew from a few dozen to a few hundred, and more.

Now, keep in mind that if you weren't in exactly the right place at the right time, you would have missed all this; mainstream press was busy covering dot-com start-ups with millions of dollars in venture capital backing. By comparison, stories about boutique publishing businesses weren't sexy enough to mention. So most people heard about this opportunity only on rare occasions, in one of two ways: they might see an occasional curiosity piece in mainstream media about a blogger-type entrepreneur who got lucky and hit it big, or they could stumble down the "make money online" rabbit hole, which was full of marketers trying to sell snake oil about getting rich on the internet.

Nonetheless, the idea that anyone with an internet connection could set up shop and reach the entire world sparked the imaginations of millions, with books like Timothy Ferriss's *4-Hour Workweek* (published in 2007) adding fuel to the fire. It wasn't just the global reach and minimal start-up costs that were so enticing; the idea of a digital product meant you could sell something that wouldn't cost a cent to fulfill. It was the pharmaceutical business model (the first pill costs a billion dollars to develop, and the second costs a penny to produce), without the up-front costs of R&D.

Publishers eventually realized that if they could make money by running ads on their sites for random products through the intermediary of Google Ads, they could make more by cutting out the middleman and advertising their own products. First there were e-books and teleseminars, and then as the technology became more robust they slowly evolved into something resembling a modern online course.

Pricing started out modest and reasonable; think of prices around $27 for an e-book and $67 for a teleseminar. Online courses felt richer and more thorough, so they sold for more, but the prices were still reasonable, maybe a few hundred dollars at most. But that didn't last; very quickly, the price of these "information products" began to climb, fueled by four factors:

- INNOVATOR PSYCHOLOGY: The thing about innovators is that they like to be on the bleeding edge; they're much less concerned about the risk of downside than they are excited by the possibility for upside, and they're perfectly happy tolerating a less-than-perfect customer experience in the process. This group of buyers tends to be price insensitive and impulsive—in other words, the easiest people in the world to whom you might sell something exciting and new.

- MINIMAL REGULATION: These early days were the Wild West of online business in general, and online courses in particular. There wasn't nearly as much restriction or regulation around what you could or couldn't do, say, or advertise, and the few limitations that did exist weren't consistently enforced. This led to a proliferation of bombastic claims of promised outcomes, with at best a very fine print at the bottom of the page to remind people that "results might not be typical."

- HIGH-DEMAND NICHES: Any marketer worth their salt knows that if you really dig down, there are only three core human drivers: the drive to make or save money, accumulate resources, and reduce risk; the drive to establish relationships and deepen human connection; and the drive to become and remain healthy, or, as some marketers like to put it, "get paid, get laid, and stay alive." Usually, marketers can't be so on-the-nose about these needs, because if they did it would raise the eyebrows of mainstream buyers and regulators—not to mention that in most industries, this low-hanging fruit of consumer demand has already been picked. But none of those conditions were true in the early days of online courses; the psychology of innovators, minimal regulation, and outsized share of voice led to hugely successful offerings like *30 Days to Mass Control Millions* and *The Annihilation Method: Seduction Blueprint.*

• OUTSIZED SHARE OF VOICE: Since these were the early days, there wasn't much by way of competition; if there was demand for a course on a particular topic and you happened to offer one, that was likely the only available option (or later, one of the few). The eager, price-insensitive innovators seeking courses to help them "get paid, get laid, and stay alive" were essentially a captive market.

These factors combined to create a very favorable and forgiving environment for would-be course creators and also rapidly accelerating price inflation, climbing over the course of a decade to the now-iconic price tag of $2,000 for a set of videos and transcripts with zero cost of fulfillment. (Why $2,000? Because it's about as much as you can charge and still get large volumes of sales without having to actually get on the phone and talk to someone; more than that usually requires the intervention of a salesperson.)

There was just one small problem with these $2,000 "information products": by and large, they didn't work. Sure, they contained some good information, and a few outlier students would experience exceptional success (which was then plastered all over the sales pages for future products). But the vast, vast majority of the people who bought these programs never experienced any meaningful result, and usually didn't even make their way through the lesson content.

Now, in fairness to the early entrepreneurs who started this trend, they meant well; they wanted to reach and help more people (which is great), and they wanted more free time to spend with their families (which is also great). So they figured, why not "teach" what they know through the internet, in a way that can reach lots of people, without having to be involved in the process? That's where the wave of information products started. The problem was that most of these people weren't teachers at all, so they just didn't understand education well enough to know what it takes to do it right.

Their implicit assumption was that all the costs that go into creating a traditional educational experience (rent, utilities, accreditation, and of course, teachers) are as superfluous to the process of learning as actual paper books are to the process of reading—but they aren't. You can read just as well on a Kindle as you can on paper (better, actually, since you can annotate, tag content, and email it to yourself at the push of a button), but you can't learn just as well from a video as you can from a good teacher.

But these accidental online entrepreneurs didn't know that, so they rolled out their information products with great success in multimillion-dollar product launches, because a great many people were eager for the outcomes being promised. And the vast majority of the people who bought these products achieved very little, which makes perfect sense; it takes a lot more than information to empower someone to do something they don't already know how to do. Even if we understand the concepts, that doesn't mean we have the ability to apply them to achieve the outcomes we care about.

Some people made fortunes in those early days and remember them as the golden age of online courses, when they could set up shop, launch something, and make a fortune with minimal effort.

Others remember those days as the dark ages, when course buyers were taken by get-rich-quick offers that fleeced them out of thousands (and sometimes tens of thousands) of dollars, without actually delivering the promised outcomes. Whatever your take on those early days, though, one thing is certain: they're long gone.

EARLY ADOPTERS AND POLARIZATION (2015–2019)

The price inflation of online courses has its roots in the difference between two competing paradigms of business. The first is a paradigm of *information*, and the second is a paradigm of *education*.

In an information business, your job is to produce something that customers want to buy, and that's it. Once someone has bought a book from a bookstore, for example, the transaction is complete and nothing further is owed to them. This isn't news to anyone; we all understand, without needing any sort of explanation, that buying a copy of *The American Red Cross First Aid and Safety Handbook* doesn't certify you in CPR, and a subscription to *The New England Journal of Medicine* doesn't make you a doctor. You can certainly learn a lot from those resources, but how much you take away from them is a personal choice for you to make that no one will hold you accountable to—not the author, not the bookstore owner, and not the publishers!

But that's not how it works when you enroll in a school or university, because they aren't publishers. Schools and universities follow an education paradigm; if you are accepted into a medical school and you're willing to invest the money, time, and effort needed to complete your studies, there is an implicit understanding and expectation that, so long as you do your part and live up to their standards and requirements, you will come out the other end with knowledge and skills certified by the diploma of a medical doctor.

That's why you can't just buy a medical degree the way that you can buy a textbook. In the context of education, there are expectations and responsibilities held by *both* parties; the student is responsible to dedicate the time and energy it takes to do the work, and the educator is responsible to facilitate the goal of learning through explanation, simulation, and coaching. The tuition doesn't buy you a medical license; it only buys you the opportunity to earn one—and it takes an enormous amount of labor, resources, and expertise to create that learning opportunity, which is why medical school tuition costs orders of magnitude more than the textbooks that contain the same body of knowledge.

So in a nutshell, information is cheap, education comes at a premium, and there are good reasons why both of those things are true. That's how things work in most of the world, but in the early days of online courses, things were different. *In that context, information was drastically overpriced, and education didn't really exist.* And for a while, that was okay, thanks to the forgiving buying habits of innovators, the lack of regulation or enforcement around what promises could actually be made by online entrepreneurs, the outsized share of voice of the course entrepreneurs who got into the game early, and those high-demand niches that were extra effective in attracting those innovators to begin with.

But things changed; as more and more people got wind of the idea that online courses were a real thing, more mature buyers started to seriously entertain them: the group that Everett Rogers would call *early adopters.* As more buyers entered the market, so did more sellers, which meant more activity, which caught the attention of regulators.

And an increasingly diverse selection of available courses led to a landscape that quickly grew richer and more competitive. (Quick aside: There were broader trends that contributed to these shifts in the landscape of learning. They're beyond the scope of this particular discussion, but if you want to learn more, please refer to Chapter 3 of my 2018 book *Leveraged Learning*, which you're welcome to buy, or read for free at LeveragedLearningBook.com.)

All of this made the mismatch between what things cost and what they were actually worth completely unsustainable. When price and value are misaligned in any market, there are only two things that can happen: either the price will adjust to reflect the value, or the value will adjust to reflect the price. In this case, both of those things happened. The market for online courses split into two completely different camps: low-cost information on one side and premium education on the other.

The course creators who stuck to just selling information but still expected to charge a premium were rudely disappointed, as the market became increasingly unwilling to pay these inflated prices. So they adapted, and it quickly became a race to the highest possible production and entertainment value (sometimes called "edutainment") at the lowest possible cost—accelerated by the growing popularity of marketplaces like Udemy (with courses officially priced at a few hundred dollars, but usually discounted to sell for just a few dozen) and publishers like MasterClass (where celebrity instructor-led courses cost about a hundred dollars). In just a few years, the days of information-only courses selling for massive price tags were quickly drawing to a close.

Were there still some exceptions, outliers, or holdouts? Yes, of course. A few topics were perceived to be rare and valuable enough for customers (however grudgingly) to continue paying a premium. And some brands were strong enough to show some staying power, but even they saw a squeeze on their margins and gradually lost ground to upstarts offering a better deal. To combat these forces, expensive information-only courses would increasingly come bundled with add-ons to justify the price, like software or coaching, and when you add coaching support to the mix, you start crossing the line that divides information from education.

That's the direction in which other course entrepreneurs chose to go: embracing the paradigm of education, and owning their responsibility to truly partner with students in pursuit of their learning goals. Those who followed this route continued to command premium prices, and found that it gradually got *easier* to do so, as the growing sophistication of the market phased the peddlers of overpriced information out of the picture. This brings us to the modern age of online courses, where the market is polarized sharply between economy information on the one hand and premium education on the other.

ONLINE COURSES GO MAINSTREAM (2020 AND ONWARD)

In January of 1848, James W. Marshall found gold in Coloma, California. The news quickly spread, and hundreds of thousands of people flocked to California from across the United States and abroad. At first, the gold was so plentiful that nuggets could be picked up off the ground. When that low-hanging fruit was exhausted, the gold seekers had to grow more sophisticated with techniques like panning and mining. Right around that time, a few entrepreneurs hit upon a realization that would make them richer than most of the gold seekers: there was much easier money to be made selling shovels than actually digging for gold!

This clichéd story is often used to caution against listening to someone promising outsized returns in whatever new opportunity they're peddling. But it is misleading on multiple levels—starting with the implication that the shovel sellers were the only real winners, but that certainly isn't true. Miners extracted more than 750,000 pounds of gold in those days, which in today's dollars would be worth over $14 billion. So that's not nothing.

Secondly, it wasn't just about the shovels; when you have enough people trying to do something, an entire cottage industry emerges to support them. Case in point: Levi Strauss & Co. was founded in 1853, selling pants to the gold miners. The stuff they had been wearing would get worn out too quickly, so the company adopted the technology of metal rivets placed on the areas of the jeans that are most likely to be pulled apart by the strain of movement, which makes the pants last longer. With over $5.8 billion in annual revenue in 2019, that's a nice chunk of change—not to mention the 15,800 people that are gainfully employed by them—that wouldn't exist if not for that initial gold rush.

And in the long run, the biggest winners of the California gold rush weren't the miners, the shovel sellers, or the entrepreneurs who built big businesses with obscure origin stories that tie back to that fateful day in 1848. The biggest winners are the Googles, Apples, and Facebooks of the world (with a combined market capitalization measured in trillions of dollars), and more broadly the 39.56 million Californians who enjoy a median household income of $71,805 (more than 20% over the national average of $59,039), whose work and lives look almost nothing like the gold rush that started it all.

Just like the California gold rush, the world of online courses has come a long way since its inception and has changed a lot in the process. Gone are the days of blue ocean markets void of competition, and gone are the days of platform loopholes that made the marketing unreasonably easy. Like any market that has moved past the innovator and early adopter stages and made it into the mainstream, it is filled with eager but discerning customers, and crowded by competitors fighting to serve them. These days, it's not surprising when a thought leader offers a course; on the contrary, it's almost weird when they *don't* have one!

Most importantly, every coach, consultant, author, speaker, or expert should know the following before setting out to build a course of their own: both the *who* and the *what* of course building have changed.

WHO makes courses has changed, and for the better. In the early days of online courses, a commonly used analogy was that of a fourth grader teaching a second grader. You don't need to know everything about a subject, just so long as you're a few steps ahead of your students, the argument would go. Some would go so far as to say that if you read five books about a subject, you know more about it than anyone but an expert, which makes you a de facto expert yourself. That latter part stretches the truth a bit for my taste, and the whole argument is ethically dubious when dealing with sensitive fields like health, or anything involving children, but by and large, the logic held back in those days, simply because the pickings were slim.

These days, the bar for required expertise is a whole lot higher, and a real shot at online course business success requires real expertise and depth in your subject area. The majority of modern online course creators are exceedingly well credentialed (case in point: of the thousands of course creators that my company has trained, 90% are college educated, and 50% hold advanced degrees). What really matters, though, isn't the credential per se, but rather the expertise, whether that comes in the form of a PhD, decades of experience, innovative research, or something else.

WHAT **courses look like has evolved considerably as well.** In the "good old days," online courses were essentially a digital version of a classroom experience: audio or video lessons housed on some sort of membership-access technology, dripping out one lesson each week for the duration of the course. These days, courses look like whatever will best serve the student, often taking a hybrid form of content that is part live and part recorded, supplemented by collaboration with peers and support from coaches. There are exceptions (which we'll discuss in the next chapter), but by and large the bar has risen considerably for what passes as a quality course experience.

It's no longer a brave new world, but that doesn't mean the window of opportunity has passed. For the right experts committed to building courses that deliver real transformation about the right topics, the golden age of online courses is just beginning, and in the next chapter, we'll explore how to go about seizing that opportunity.

Chapter 2
YOUR COURSE
AND YOUR BUSINESS

"Good fortune is what happens when opportunity meets planning."
-Thomas Edison

IN EARLY 2005, Michael and Lily Idov opened a small café on New York's Lower East Side. They sold authentic Vienna roast (lighter and sweeter than conventional espresso). The décor was charming and the presentation was beautiful—each coffee beverage served on shiny metal trays with a glass of water and a chocolate cookie. It was a lovely concept, and six months later it was out of business. This wasn't a function of poor management—in Michael's own words, writing about the experience for Slate, it was an "inevitability."

It all comes down to the math. When you figure the cost of rent and labor against the value of a sale times the twenty to twenty-five people a "cozy" café can hold, you arrive at an inescapably money-losing proposition. There are two common ways to get around the math; you can augment your sales with people who take their coffee to go, or the proprietors can save on labor costs by doing all the work themselves. Which isn't a real solution, because there's only so long that a business can be subsidized by the unpaid labor of its employers.

The Idovs had to learn the same lesson as every other entrepreneur (hopefully before running out of money): that a great product and a great business aren't the same thing, and that businesses work when you find the right way for the product to fit into the mix. Let's continue with another coffee example.

Starbucks, Nespresso, and Lavazza are all coffee companies, but they have almost nothing in common other than the coffee!

Online courses are products in the same way that coffee is a product. Some are incredibly good, some are average, and some are subpar. But it's more than the quality of the product that determines whether it will be a winning proposition for the entrepreneur who pours heart and soul into it. The bigger determinant of success is how the product of an online course fits into the broader picture of the online course business.

WHY PASSIVE INCOME IS (PROBABLY) A FANTASY

The landmark work of James O. Prochaska and Carlo DiClemente is their "Transtheoretical Model," which is sometimes referred to as the "Stages of Change." According to the theory, people spend quite a while warming up to the idea of making a change (like quitting smoking) or starting something new (like building an online course business). During that time of "Precontemplation" and "Contemplation" (which precedes "Preparation" and "Action"), we essentially compare and contrast life as it is today (e.g., a smoker who lives with chronic emphysema and everything smelling like cigarettes) with life as it could be if we actually were to make a change (live healthy, smell great). The thing is, we don't actually know what the future holds. Sometimes reality ends up looking strikingly like we imagined it would, and other times it turns out to be very different, depending on how well-informed our guesses were in the first place.

Over the past decade, I've supported thousands of coaches, consultants, authors, speakers, and experts on their journeys from online course "Precontemplation" through "Action" and to success. In some ways, they end up exactly where they imagined; they really do impact more people, make more money, and feel more free. But in other ways, they discover that their guesses were woefully uneducated, which makes sense, because they tend to be informed by a hangover from the course gold rush of the early 2000s! The imagined picture usually looks something like this: "I'll take my book or keynote presentation and create a course version of the same content. Then I'll set it up online, and people will buy it—that's my ticket to (limitless!) passive income."

These days, it doesn't often work out that way, and not just because turning a book or keynote presentation into a course generally makes for a pretty bad course (more on that in Chapters 3 and 5). The challenge runs deeper, to a fundamental contradiction between the vision of passive income and the reality of most aspiring course entrepreneurs.

That's because, for most people, the words *passive income* conjure up a vague picture of...

1. ...STRANGERS ON THE INTERNET automagically discovering something you've built...
2. ...FINDING YOUR MESSAGE COMPELLING ENOUGH to pull out their credit cards...
3. ...AND THEN GETTING EVERYTHING that they paid for...

...all without you having to lift a finger, or maybe even be awake! (There's an alluring mystique to the idea of "making money while you sleep"!) And sure, you might have to work hard to build the perpetual money machine, but once it's built you can just "set it and forget it," or so the fantasy goes. Except that in real life, it doesn't usually work that way, because real passive income requires that two very particular stars align, which aren't often seen together: low price and high volume.

Low price is necessary because if the price is high, neither the sale nor the fulfillment can be passive. On the sales side, if you go over a certain price threshold the cycles become more complex and often require the intervention of a salesperson. And on the fulfillment side, the more people pay, the more they expect to receive, including support, interactivity, coaching, and the like. Now, there's nothing wrong with any of that, and there are great businesses to be built that include a more involved sales process and coaching of customers once they buy, but while they can be rewarding and lucrative, they don't usually fit the image conjured up by the word *passive*. So passive income requires a low price.

But a low price isn't enough; it also requires high volume, because if the price is low and you want the income to add up to a meaningful amount, you need to make up for that low price with high volume—low price times low volume might be passive, but it won't be much income! So we also need high volume; in other words, we need to sell a whole lot of courses! But that is often easier said than done, and to understand why, we need to take a short digression into the world of unit economics.

UNIT ECONOMICS: THE SECRET KEYS TO SUCCESSFUL BUSINESS

Before Stephen Hawking published his classic *A Brief History of Time* in 1988, his publisher gave him a stern warning: "every equation that you include in this book will cut its readership in half." That warning weighed heavily on me as I wrote the section you're about to read, because there's no way to talk about unit economics without bringing at least a tiny bit of math into the conversation. So please, bear with me for the next couple of pages, and then we'll be done with the math.

So what are unit economics? Fundamentally, they're the nuts and bolts of what makes businesses successful. If you've ever tried to raise money from investors—or even if you like to watch shows like *Shark Tank* or listen to podcasts like *The Pitch*—you know that a charismatic founder's cool idea is just the beginning. Once you've got their attention, they'll want to dig deeper.

The first thing investors want to understand is your *contribution profit*. To find that, we start with the price of whatever it is you're selling, take away the cost of acquiring the customer (i.e., direct sales and marketing costs) and the cost of fulfilling on the sale (i.e., production, shipping, and support). Your contribution profit is whatever amount is left over after those variable costs are taken out. Now take that contribution profit and multiply it by all the sales you make. If you get a number that is smaller than all your fixed costs (like rent and salaries), you're in trouble. That's what happened to Michael and Lily Idov's café, simply because they couldn't serve the volume of customers that they would have needed to turn a profit. If it's more or less on par, you'll live to fight another day. And if you have a lot of money left over, that means you've got a great business.

(Some Silicon Valley investors like to believe that unit economics aren't that important in the early stages of a company's growth, and sometimes they're right, but it's only a matter of time before the math catches up to you. That's why Uber stock has lost a third of its value since its IPO.)

In the context of an online course business, a good rule of thumb is that for the math to work, the price of your course will split into three more or less equal parts: one-third customer acquisition, one-third fulfillment, and one-third contribution profit. So if you're selling a $1,000 course, you can afford to spend about $333 on attracting the student and $333 on delivering a great experience to them (more on that in Chapter 5), and you'll have $333 left over to contribute to all your other regular expenses.

Okay, so that's it for our digression. Now that we know what unit economics are, we can talk about why they make the passive income fantasy out of reach for most course entrepreneurs. Remember that passive income requires two things: low price (otherwise it isn't passive) and high volume (otherwise it isn't much income). But we're also constrained by unit economics, with a rule of thumb that we can spend about a third of the retail price (which is already low) on acquiring the customer. A third of a low price is very little money, and customers are usually expensive to acquire. Here's how you figure out the number for you:

1. HOW MANY LEADS DO YOU NEED to get your message in front of to get one sale?
2. HOW MUCH DOES IT COST (in dollars, or value of time) to attract one lead?

Multiply the answers to both questions, and you get your *customer acquisition cost* (CAC). So, for example, if you run ads on Facebook and it costs you $5 to get a lead (which is on the low end of reasonable), and your regular process converts one out of every fifty leads into a customer (which is probably optimistic), then this is the math:

$$\text{\$5/lead} \times 50 \text{ leads} = \text{\$250 customer acquisition cost}$$

And if you can spend roughly a third of your retail price to acquire a customer, then that means you'd need to charge $750 to make the math work on those Facebook ads, which is probably more than you can charge and still have the experience be completely passive. So that doesn't work. The only way you can make the passive income dream a reality is if you can find an unusually cheap way of attracting students.

UNUSUALLY CHEAP WAYS OF ATTRACTING STUDENTS

The good news is that there *are* ways of attracting students very inexpensively, which is why passive income isn't a total myth. But unfortunately, most of those ways are unattainable for most course creators. See if they feel attainable to you:

- EARLY MOVER ADVANTAGE. Early movers on the right opportunities get a whole lot of advantages. If we're talking markets (e.g., you teach the first internet course on weight loss), then you get in before anyone is there to compete. If we're talking platforms (e.g., you're on Facebook before anybody else), then it's easier to build your following and your ads run for cheap. The problem is that these days, most markets are mature, and your only shot at being an early mover is to take a chance on the social media world's hot flavor of the week—TikTok, anyone?

- PRIME PLACEMENT. There are places where loads of your ideal prospects are already hanging out, like the top of search platforms like Google, YouTube, and Amazon, or the home pages of course marketplaces like Udemy, Highbrow, or Skillshare. If you have the connections or positioning to land one of those coveted spots, it will very inexpensively expose loads of new leads to your message and offer. Unfortunately, there are far more people vying to secure those spots than there are spots to be had, so it's pretty competitive.

- CELEBRITY STATUS. Being a celebrity—whether A-list globally or B-list in your own industry—makes everything easier. You're more likely to get the prime placements on platform sites, because they want to showcase their association with you. Your ad costs go down, because people are more likely to want to know what you're up to. Oh, and you've very likely amassed an audience of tens or hundreds of thousands of people. That's the Kylie Cosmetics success plan—going from zero to a billion dollars in five years with twelve employees and no marketing budget, thanks to Kylie Jenner's over 150 million followers.

- BUYING IN BULK. There's a dirty little secret that advertising gurus don't like to tell you when they promise that "you, too, can turn $1 into $10 by following our system": that the prices they pay for ads and the prices you pay for ads aren't the same, because they're buying in bulk. Yes, they might be buying leads on Facebook for just a few dollars, but that's because they're buying thousands of them every day. If you're just dipping your toe in the water (which Facebook and other ad platforms and media companies loosely define as spending less than six figures annually), they'll charge you a multiple of that bulk price.

- SUBSIDIZED ACQUISITION. Remember how I said that you can spend about a third of your list price to acquire the customer? Well, there's an exception to that rule in cases where you know the customer is going to buy more than just the one course. Let's say, for example, that in addition to my $300 course, I also sell a $30,000 mastermind, and I expect that one out of every hundred course buyers will upgrade to the next level. In that case, I can afford to spend twice as much to acquire the customer (a third of the course price, plus a third of a hundredth of the mastermind price).

So yes, if you blew up on Facebook before it was cool, control the top search rankings on Google and YouTube, have major celebrity status and a hundred thousand raving fans, can afford to buy traffic in bulk, or can overspend on marketing because you know you'll make it up on the back-end, then sure, adding some passive income to your business is no big deal.

But what if you don't have those unfair advantages playing in your favor? After all, most of the coaches, consultants, authors, speakers, and experts who set out to build online courses just don't, or at least not when they're getting started. In that case, the passive income fantasy is just that: a fantasy. But that doesn't mean a thriving online course business that creates leverage, freedom, and impact is out of reach. It'll just look a bit different than it did in 2005.

THE OPPORTUNITY FOR MODERN ONLINE COURSES

The biggest change since the early days of online courses is that back in the early 2000s, you didn't actually need a business. You could have a mediocre course paired with access to unreasonably cheap leads, and they could create income for you, automagically. That was real passive income.

These days, an online course can't magically create passive income (meaning that you earn money while doing nothing), but an online course *business* can absolutely create leverage (meaning that you get more by doing less). And there are three broad roles that courses can play in that business: they can support, they can augment, or they can transform.

COURSES THAT SUPPORT

To say that weddings are important would be an understatement; these (hopefully) once-in-a-lifetime events are intense, emotional, stressful, and wonderful—so much so that in the U.S. alone the wedding industry is reportedly worth over $50 billion each year. But important as weddings are, they're just a single day in what will hopefully be a long and prosperous relationship. Before the wedding, there is dating, courtship, and engagement, in which the couple explores their attraction and alignment. Then, after the wedding, there's the marriage, with all the ups and downs that come with a lifetime of shared experiences.

Similarly, as entrepreneurs, we tend to fixate on the moment in which prospects decide to become customers by trading their hard-earned cash for our product or service, and for good reason; it's a very important moment! But just as weddings are only a tiny slice of the relationships that they cement, the moment of purchase is only a small part of the life cycle a customer traverses, as the focus of the relationship shifts from awareness, to engagement, and then to retention. In the context of online courses, there is certainly money to be made by building a business around selling them, and we'll get to that shortly. But just as large is the opportunity to build courses that support all the rest of the customer life cycle.

Before the moment of purchase, courses can support the marketing journey by attracting leads, demonstrating expertise, and delivering customer education that teaches the things that make customers ready to buy. Examples include courses that help people understand the need for whatever else it is that you're selling and create an opportunity for the most engaged prospects to rise to the top, so you can focus your sales energy on them.

And after the moment of sale, courses can support the customer experience by teaching how to use (and get the most out of) the product or service, or automating some of the more repetitive elements of customer support (so rather than individually answering the same question asked by 200 different people, you create training materials that circumvent the question altogether).

Whether it's before or after the point of purchase, courses that support often fit well into businesses that sell things with a higher customer lifetime value, like software or high-end services. Whereas the core offerings that they support are pricier, the courses themselves tend to be short and simple (more information than true education), and are usually free or low-cost (which works, because they are essentially subsidized by the broader offer that they support).

COURSES THAT AUGMENT

On October 19, 1896, the world's very first movie theater opened to the public in Buffalo, New York. The 72-seat theater was an instant hit, with over 200,000 admissions in the first year alone. More theaters slowly opened over the following decades as the technology became more accessible, and the selection of available movies improved. Then, in the 1920s, the movie business exploded, as independent promoters and movie studios raced to build the most lavish, elaborate, and attractive theaters. These are the humble beginnings of an industrial complex with tentacles extending far and wide: concession sales (think popcorn and sodas in theaters), home video purchases (on VHS, then DVD, and now streaming), merchandise (from Mickey Mouse to My Little Pony, and everything in between), resorts and theme parks (like Walt Disney World), and a whole lot more. Once a customer existed, there were many more things to sell them. Of course, this isn't unique to the film industry; cafés sell pastries, hotels offer Wi-Fi (for a small fee), electronics come with optional insurance, and McDonald's asks if you'd like fries with that.

Many businesses have the same opportunity to augment their offerings through online courses, especially if they're in the business of expertise. Coaches, consultants, authors, speakers, and experts all have the opportunity to supplement their work with a course that better supports the behavior change that their clients so desperately want. For example, speakers might offer a course as an add-on to the talk that they deliver to organizations. And coaches who work with the senior members of a team can create courses that their clients can use with the people under them in the organization.

Now, this can be a relatively small augmentation, adding as little as 10–30% to an entrepreneur's bottom line, which isn't bad given that it actually is fairly passive, if you consider that the rest of the business is going to operate either way. Or it can be a massive one that ends up being a bigger profit center than the original service. Case in point: Disney theme parks and resorts were an augmentation that came after the movie business, but today the parks gross almost double the revenue generated by Disney's studio entertainment division (according to their annual report). By the same token, course entrepreneurs sometimes find that they have to continue doing what they've been doing as the engine that keeps the business in motion, but that the majority of their revenues (and especially profits) come from their online courses.

Courses that augment an existing business can be anywhere on the pricing spectrum. In some cases, they are very inexpensive (which works, because the rest of the business is subsidizing the customer acquisition). And in other cases, they can be quite costly (which works, because they're still a bargain relative to the price of the core offering, which is an order of magnitude larger). Where these courses sit on the information vs. education spectrum will vary depending on the price point, but it is important that they deliver a meaningful transformation since they end up being seen as part of the transformation that the expert is offering, which means their brand reputation is on the line. I'll share more on what makes for truly transformative courses in Chapters 3 and 5.

COURSES THAT TRANSFORM

Imagine that you're a skilled screenwriter who wants to help your peers refine their craft, or a marriage and family therapist who wants to help couples bring the spark back to their relationship. The low price/high volume "passive income" part of the market is already cornered by people like Aaron Sorkin (who wrote for shows like *The West Wing* and movies like *A Few Good Men*, and whose course goes for about $100 on MasterClass) and Esther Perel (author of *Mating in Captivity* and *The State of Affairs*, whose *Rekindling Desire* course is listed on her website for $199). Unless you have their celebrity status, plus the built-in reach of MasterClass or the audience that grows out of multiple best-selling books, TED talks, and speaking engagements, how can you compete?

Pining for a past romantic partner can blind you to the merits of the people sitting across from you right now. Similarly, lamenting the long-gone opportunities of the online course gold rush of the early 2000s can blind us to the best business models to be capitalized on today. No, the passive income opportunity is no longer available to most course creators, but there's a new opportunity—bigger and more exciting—that is now available. Back in the day, most aspiring screenwriters and frustrated couples didn't even know that online courses were an option. But now they do, precisely because Sorkin, Perel, and every other expert of their stature (as well as the platforms with which they collaborate) have leveraged their reach and resources to spread the word. Many thousands (if not tens or hundreds of thousands) of people have taken these courses in every industry and niche, and a good portion wants to go even further.

That desire to go further is the biggest opportunity for course builders to tap into. Neither the "instructors" on MasterClass (like Sorkin) nor the independent celebrity experts (like Perel) have the time, bandwidth, or financial incentives to work closely enough with students to support a deeper and more meaningful transformation, except maybe through private practice. So where do the growing masses of students who want more than a few-hundred-dollar course can provide but don't have the resources or opportunity to work directly with the expert go?

The exciting answer is that they go to you: the qualified and competent coach, consultant, speaker, author, or expert who is great at what you do, has a lot of expertise to impart, but doesn't have the celebrity status or reach of the biggest names in your field. You have the freedom and luxury to build courses that deliver real transformation and sell them for a premium (think thousands of dollars). Multiply thousands of dollars by hundreds or thousands of students, and you'll have a business generating hundreds of thousands or millions of dollars in gross annual revenue. This isn't passive, but it is very lucrative—enough so to create an abundance of leverage, freedom, and impact.

These sorts of courses tend to go further than just delivering information ("teaching about"), and focus on real transformation ("teaching to"). They supplement the training materials (video, audio, text, etc.) with coaching and interactivity, which can be delivered by the course creators, or by coaches who work for them (which is still very profitable, given the unit economics of these sorts of courses). The rest of what I have to share with you in the coming chapters applies to all kinds of courses and course businesses but is primarily geared at this opportunity: to create courses that are truly transformative, both for your students and for you.

Chapter 3

FROM GOOD IDEA TO WINNING COURSE

"Be not afraid of growing slowly, be only afraid of standing still."

-CONFUCIUS

ONLINE COURSES CHANGED MY LIFE twice: first as a student when I learned the skills I needed to begin growing my business, and then as an instructor when I was able to create leverage, freedom, and impact in my business and life. I shared my story at the very beginning of this book, and it's all true, but there's a chapter that I left out. You see, the very first online course I created didn't do well at all.

It started with a brilliant idea, one that I was sure would be a huge hit. I went into my "Batcave" and spent substantial amounts of time, money, and energy putting my course together. I kept tweaking and improving it, trying to make it absolutely perfect. Finally, the big day arrived, and I launched it to the world—certain it would make a huge impact, and earn a lot of money in the process. But the sales never came. To say that it was a giant disappointment would be an understatement; I literally spent thousands of hours before making a cent, and in the entire lifetime of that course it didn't sell so many as fifty copies.

Thankfully, I learned from the experience and didn't make the same mistake again. The next three courses that I launched were all blockbuster successes, proving that the learning experience, while painful, was absolutely worthwhile. With the first of those three courses, which I launched in 2012, it took only 60 hours of work to go from start to first dollar earned. With the second (launched in 2013) it took only 30 hours, and with the third (launched in 2015) it took only 20 hours. And it's not just about speed to market either—the quality of the courses kept getting better!

THE POWER OF PILOTING

What I learned through hard experience—and what I teach the coaches, consultants, speakers, authors, and experts that my company trains—is that we can't help but approach course building (like any new endeavor) with a set of assumptions. Those assumptions are about what exactly people want to pay to learn from you, what prior knowledge they'll bring to the table, what they'll find most challenging, what the best way is to get each point across, and so on. And some of those assumptions are bound to be wrong. In some cases (because of inexperience or sheer bad luck), the majority of your assumptions turn out to be wrong. And in other cases (when you have a lot of experience teaching about your topic and working with your target audience), only a small portion of the assumptions turns out to be wrong.

The trouble is that building a successful online course business is more like building a bridge than writing a paper; if you get 90% of the work right on a paper for school, you'll get an A, but if you get 90% of the work right when building a bridge, you'll get a lawsuit. So even if your assumptions are off by as little as 10–20%, it's a problem. And there's no way of knowing in advance which 10–20% of your assumptions will turn out to be the wrong ones.

The only way to know for sure is to test. Your first course, which we call a *pilot* course, should be designed to validate a few basic assumptions as quickly and inexpensively as possible: quickly, so that you can pivot and iterate rapidly as the situation calls for, and inexpensively, so as to minimize the risk to the entrepreneur. It's the Silicon Valley dictum of "first make it work, then make it better."

Neither of these goals—speed and low cost—are met by the ambitions of most first-time course creators, who want to teach everything about everything that relates to their topic area and wind up with plans for a massive six-month or yearlong course. That sort of course takes ages to produce, which means a very long timeline to gaining real knowledge about whether the market actually wants it. Adding insult to injury, the broad focus of such a mega-course means that while it's somewhat valuable to a lot of people, it isn't very valuable to anyone, which makes it very hard to sell. And if the course does somehow attract students, and those students struggle to get to the finish line (which is very likely on the first iteration of any course), the expansive scope makes it very difficult to diagnose what exactly went wrong and to discover what can be done differently or better in the future.

To avoid all that, and set ourselves up to learn the lessons we need in time to inform future decisions, we start with a pilot. This isn't the final, extended magnum opus that you might one day create.

Rather, it's the minimum viable version for you to get outside validation that you're on the right track. And through it you can validate demand for the course you want to offer, and co-create a transformative learning experience that is worth paying for.

The primary goal for launching your pilot is to validate demand for your offer. When you enter a new space or try to build something for the first time, your priority should be to gather information—to validate that people are willing and eager to pay for what you want to do, in the format that you want to provide. In other words, you need to find out if people actually *want* what you're selling. This validation happens in stages, culminating with the pilot itself, and will help you avoid wasted effort.

In the medium term, you'll build a track record of success, particularly if you're entering a new space or branching out in a new direction. In that case, one of the biggest challenges is showing proof that you can help people in the way you say you can. A pilot is a great way to generate proof of concept and build a track record of successfully selling and delivering your content (more details on selling in Chapter 4).

Having this track record will be important for two future scenarios: First, the experience of supporting your students and delivering on your promises will lead to satisfied customers, which will in turn lead to case studies and testimonials. These will be priceless as you continue to grow and scale your business. Second, it puts you in a stronger position down the line when you're ready to approach other leaders in your industry who might become joint venture partners and help promote your products and extend your reach.

As an added bonus, over time, the piloting process has a way of creeping into other areas of business as well. In the beginning, you might focus on validating your very first pilot idea. But once you have that experience under your belt, you can apply the piloting framework to additional ideas. You might choose to run a second pilot on the same topic, or run a new pilot on a completely different idea. Before long, you might use the piloting methodology on other services as well, such as coaching, consulting, group calls, or even live events. The methodology can be used over and over again throughout your entrepreneurial career.

Let's turn now to the process you can follow to get your pilot course moving.

But first, a quick word about outsourcing the development of your course. I frequently get asked whether there's a way for someone to just "build my course for me," and I completely understand why this seems like such an appealing possibility for busy professionals and business owners. And if you're building the sort of low-price, high-volume course that promises passive income for those who are positioned in such a way that they can actually make it happen, it can work.

But if you're looking to create something truly transformative that commands and justifies a premium price, there really isn't a way of doing this that doesn't involve rolling up your sleeves and getting involved. Because it's so essential to run a piloting process and have direct contact with participants yourself, attempting to outsource course development is likely to lead to a course that doesn't meet your audience's needs or reflect well on your brand.

STEP 1: VALIDATE DEMAND

The first step in developing your pilot course is to establish that there's actual demand for your course idea—that customers want to buy what you're planning to create. This might sound blindingly obvious, but unfortunately too many course creators skip over this step. They wind up designing a course that sounds good in concept but doesn't actually resonate with customers. It doesn't sell, and all the course creation effort is wasted.

So how do you validate demand for your course idea? The right approach depends on how well you already know your market and industry. If you already have a great deal of experience teaching the subject matter, and you've successfully sold coaching, workshops, in-person events, or other programs, then you may already have your finger on the pulse of your customer's needs. You can move faster to define your course idea and start preselling it (step 4). That moment of sale will always be the ultimate validation point, as there's no clearer indication of a viable market for your course than people who are actually willing to pay for it.

Industry experience can lead to insights about what people want and need, and these insights are a great starting point. Be warned, though: Experience can also create blinders. The deeper your experience, the more embedded your assumptions are, and the more likely it is that you'll miss some dimension of your market's real needs and challenges.

Remember that launching a successful pilot is not just about creating the course you think will be the most useful or solve the biggest problem. It's about creating something that serves the actual stated need of the people you're looking to serve (who probably don't have your sophistication with the subject matter, and by extension your ability to correctly diagnose what they actually need). In order to make the offer compelling, you'll need to refine your basic idea so you can talk to people about it in a way that's meaningful and emotionally engaging. That's why it is so important to discover what people in your market really want and are willing to buy—in their own words.

My team and I teach aspiring course creators to explore their customers' needs and language through some simple research that involves the most basic of technologies: the telephone. It's simple. Make a list of ten to twenty people you know who are connected to the sort of student you want to serve, and call them.

After some initial small talk, start the conversation with a very brief explanation of what you're up to and why you're asking them to take this time with you. This shouldn't take long at all, just a couple of minutes, and be careful about leading them in a certain direction, or seeding assumptions they may not already hold. After all, you want *their* perspective—not your own perspective reflected back to you. So, without pointing to specific product directions, ask questions such as the following:

- What is your biggest struggle with [topic]?
- Why do you think it's such a challenge? What causes the problem?
- What solutions have you tried? What results did you see?
- In a perfect world, what would be available to solve this problem?

The idea is to be sensitive but to also get as close to the root of the issue as possible. It's often in these moments when you're quiet and actively listening that the most helpful problem language comes out and core insights are found. And always remember to note their exact language; try to avoid summarizing or paraphrasing what they're saying, because you want the actual words they use.

After each call, take a few moments to consolidate your biggest observations and "aha" moments. Then once you've done a few calls, step back and reflect on what you've learned. What are the key problems and needs you could help people with through a course? These insights should be the foundation of determining the scope for your pilot, which we'll discuss next.

This research will help you collect additional evidence that there is a demand for your idea. It will also help you home in on a specific component of the general problem or desire—including the language your contacts use to describe it—that you can address in a short pilot course. You will also decide on a specific outcome or transformation you can facilitate for your participants.

Now, remember that the point is to get a deep, personal look at your topic and industry from other people's perspectives. You want to learn how they see the problem you're looking to solve, why they think it's a problem at all, and what they believe the root causes are. One key here is that you need to hear their voices, and ideally see their faces, through video calls or in-person meetings. That way you can get a sense of their emotional responses as you talk. This will help you decide whether you should pursue a line of discussion further or switch tracks to something that may yield more fruit. If a few of your contacts absolutely can't find the time, email is better than nothing, but you will get much better and richer information from a live call, so that's how the majority of your conversations should be conducted.

STEP 2: IDENTIFY MINIMUM VIABLE SCOPE

The next step to finalizing your pilot idea is to make sure the focus and scope are as narrow as they can be. We do this by using a concept called the *minimum viable outcome*, which is basically about determining the smallest scope for your pilot that will still create an outcome your customers will be happy with. This is an important step, because for many aspiring course creators the instinct is to be as generous and helpful with their knowledge as they can be. So your initial vision for a pilot might be a lot longer and more complex than it needs to be.

But you have to remember the reason for piloting in the first place—you're validating a lot of assumptions, or hopes, including that people want to pay for what you're selling, that you can deliver the outcomes you're promising, and that you have enough passion for the topic to sustain you through the challenges of growing a business. It's a lot easier to validate these things when you keep the focus specific and narrow. Also, people taking your pilot generally don't want to become experts in your field. They just want the outcomes you're promising them. So teach them only what they absolutely need to know to get a result.

An easy way to zero in on an appropriate level of focus involves a thought exercise about a short plane ride from New York to Chicago. Imagine, if you will, that you arrive at the airport, go through security, and board your plane. You find your seat and fasten your seat belt. After the flight attendant has pointed out the door you just came in through and explained how to fasten the seat belt you've already fastened, the plane takes off and you're on your way. Just as the plane starts taxiing down the runway, you start chatting with the person sitting next to you. You immediately hit it off, and learn that they are your ideal student and in dire need of your help. You'd love to just give them access to your course, but you haven't created it yet. And you've got a busy schedule, so you just don't have time to help them one-on-one. This leaves you with the length of the flight, which is just over two hours long, to teach them as much as you can to provide that help and transform their lives. So what would you teach in those two hours that would create the biggest impact?

This thought exercise is useful in arriving at a focus for your pilot course because it crystallizes your thinking around the minimum viable outcome that you can deliver that would still be meaningfully impactful to your students. You can then test your hypothesis in relatively short order, and maximize your chances of success by co-creating as much of the curriculum as possible with your actual students. Here are a few questions you can ask yourself to see if your focus is narrow enough:

1. HOW LONG WILL MY PILOT HAVE TO BE IN ORDER TO DELIVER ON THIS PROMISE? There are some exceptions, but in most cases pilots shouldn't be more than four to six weeks long. If you need much longer to deliver on your promise, you might want to scale back the scope.

2. IF SOMEONE WERE TO START MY PILOT BUT QUIT AFTER A MONTH, WOULD THEY SEE ANY BENEFITS? If so, what would those be? And how could you cram the most possible benefits into those first four weeks? Can you make those the only benefits offered in the pilot?

3. IF WHATEVER YOU'RE DOING FOR THEM IS YIELDING RESULTS, WHAT WOULD BE THE FIRST BIG MILESTONE THEY WOULD HIT THAT WOULD GIVE THEM A REAL VISCERAL SENSE THAT THIS IS WORKING? If that milestone is so compelling, can you make it the entire promise of your pilot?

The point of these questions is to help you narrow down the scope and focus of what you'll offer. This makes it easier for you to deliver on your promise, and also creates a tighter and more focused promise that your audience is more likely to get excited about.

STEP 3: PLAN YOUR PILOT

Before you can go any further, you need a plan for how many lessons your pilot will span and what you'll teach in each of them. It is important to create this plan, and just as important to keep it short—to a single-page outline, if possible. Now, a one-page outline may seem unreasonably sparse, especially in contrast to what many first-time course creators do, which is to spend months mapping out detailed scripts of every word they are going to say. But a long and detailed script is a terrible idea, for a couple of reasons.

First of all, it isn't likely to create a good experience for your students. Even if you know your subject matter, that doesn't mean you know how to teach it in this kind of course format, because you haven't done it before. Since this is a new experience, you don't know where your students might be confused, or get stuck, or need help. The more rigid and detailed your curriculum plan, the harder it will be to diverge from it when your students need you to. On the other hand, a co-created curriculum and learning experience (as you'll learn how to deliver later in this chapter, and the next one) will be a lot better for your students, and for you too.

Beyond these disadvantages to your students, the business logistics of developing a longer script mean that the longer you spend preparing, the longer it will take you to launch. The longer it takes you to launch, the more inertia can tend to set in, and the more likely it is that life will get in the way.

The solution is to prepare in advance only what you need to enroll your co-creating students, which can usually be achieved by mapping out what you intend to teach in a single page. This outline should take you only a few hours to create; make a list of the big topics that you need to cover, and each of them will be a lesson. Under each of those topics, add a handful of bullets about the specific things you will talk about. This is enough of an outline for you to be able to sell your pilot course with, and once you've sold it, you will spend a little more time fleshing out each lesson, and perhaps designing some high-level handouts, worksheets, and other materials.

Now, you might feel that this is scant preparation, and you'd be right—except that you're already coming to the table with a wealth of expertise. Remind yourself of your expertise in this subject matter. All you need at this stage is a high-level overview of what concepts you will teach to your students and in what order. The specifics of how to teach them are best co-created with your students live, in real-time, informed by the in-the-moment reactions and responses of your students. Detailed scripts or slides prepared in advance of that input are unlikely to be well aligned with what your students will actually need in the moment.

If this makes you a little uncomfortable, that's okay; remember the importance of stepping out of your comfort zone. It can be uncomfortable, but this method allows you to adjust, pivot, and iterate to create the best experience for your students. It will also inform the creation of your final (non-pilot) course further down the line, which is when you'll take everything that you learned in the pilot and turn it into high-quality videos and other materials.

The one-page outline is all you need to attract students, and once you have them you'll be able to develop the curriculum with them in real-time. Counterintuitively, this real-time development is critical to the creation of a curriculum that best serves your students. We'll explore that further, but first, you'll need students to teach.

STEP 4: PRE-SELL YOUR COURSE

Having validated demand for your course, identified minimum viable scope, and created a one-page plan, it is now time to presell students into your pilot. That's right—you'll enroll students, even though the course doesn't exist yet. We'll explore the specifics of *how* to do it in Chapter 4, but first let's explore *why* it is such a critical part of the process. Basically, it gives you a good response to the most challenging objection-in-the-form-of-a-question that you'll face when selling a brand-new course: "Who has gone through the course already, and what have their results been?"

Of course, the answers are "nobody" and "nothing," because the course is brand-new. This is a huge disadvantage that you need to overcome, and the process of pre-selling is so important because it acts as a special bit of marketing jujitsu, turning that weakness into a strength. To understand why that is, we must travel back in time to July of 2012, when Michael I. Norton of Harvard Business School, Daniel Mochon of Tulane University, and Dan Ariely of Duke University published an article in the *Journal of Consumer Psychology*, describing a phenomenon that they called the *IKEA effect*.

They discovered this phenomenon by conducting a series of experiments in which a group of test subjects were given the task of building or creating something. They ran experiments where the participants built things out of LEGO blocks, or folded origami figures, or assembled IKEA boxes—which is where the experiment got its name. Once the participants were finished, they were asked how much they would pay for whatever it was that they built. Then the researchers got a new group of people and showed them what the previous group had built, and asked what they would be willing to pay for those same objects.

In essence, they studied—through scientific and statistically valid methods—how valuable people perceive things that they make to be compared to things made by others. The results showed unequivocally that people place a lot more value on things they were involved in creating than on things made by somebody else. And the more involved they are in the creation, the more they value what is ultimately produced.

This research has important implications about your pilot courses: both how you will deliver them, and especially the way in which you will enroll paying students (and overcome any lack of marketing ability or resources). Consider, for a moment, the relationship you have with most products and services you see advertised. It's hard, isn't it? The truth is that we don't have much of a relationship with most of the things we think about buying, because whatever it is, somebody else created it for their own reasons. We hope that it'll be helpful and valuable to us, but if we find something that could be a little better or cheaper, then we'll just go with that option instead.

If you've already bought it, though, it's a different story. Your experience with what you've bought, and its impact on your life, create a narrative that makes it special and unique—and if the experience has been positive, then you'll probably be loyal to the product. Maybe you've heard the marketing truism that a customer who has already bought something from you is eight times more likely to buy again than a stranger is to make their first purchase. Well, that's because of the narrative of relationship that your customers have with you, which strangers don't. It's the Cocktail Party Effect, applied to business. You know how when you're at a party where there are a dozen conversations going on, it's hard to focus on any one of them? But the moment someone mentions you, your ears and brain zero in on that conversation and ignore all the rest. That's what co-creation does for you and your business: it makes your audience a part of the narrative of your offer's creation. As you continue to share the story, they perk up and pay attention because it's their story too.

That's the power of co-creating with your prospects and pre-selling your pilot; it makes your audience part of the creation of your pilot course, which gives you an advantage even stronger than a list of paying customers. Incidentally, this process can really be applied only if you're willing and able to start with smaller pilots—by asking your prospects for their input before you create your offer, and then asking the people who sign up for more input as you deliver your pilot to them so you can make it better. This puts the IKEA effect into play by making your whole audience a part of creating your offer, regardless of whether they buy your pilot (which many will) or they aren't ready yet; either way, they'll be bound to you in a powerful way that most other businesses just can't compete with, and that sets you up for success in the short term and in the long term.

STEP 5: DELIVER

Let's return for a moment to our story about the flight from New York to Chicago. However you pass the time on the flight, there's no question in your mind that the plane will in fact land in Chicago, within a small margin of error of the initial promised landing time. You'd never worry about the plane ending up in Minneapolis, Nashville, or anywhere else that isn't the destination on your ticket.

In fact, I'll bet that if at some point during the flight, the captain were to announce that you were heading in the wrong direction, you'd be surprised, and maybe even shocked or worried. But here's the really shocking part: Even though the captain doesn't make those announcements, the plane is heading in the wrong direction for over 90% of the flight. You know how the in-flight channel with the map that shows your progress makes it look like you're flying in a straight line? Well, it actually zigzags, with constant little adjustments. The captain never bothers to mention it, because it happens hundreds of times along the way, and it's totally normal; course corrections to adjust for variances in air pressure, new information about flight traffic, or the changing weight of the plane as fuel is consumed are all just normal parts of getting from point A to point B.

Now, other than giving you something to think about the next time you get on a plane, what does this have to do with online education or building courses? Just as with flying a plane to the destination you want to reach, the key to creating an excellent (and profitable) educational experience is having a lot of checkpoints along the way that tell you whether you're on track, and if not, allow you to course correct (no pun intended). That way, you're dramatically more likely to arrive at an end product that will truly support your students in achieving their success.

The actual delivery will be pretty simple and straightforward; you'll connect with your students to deliver your first lesson, and check in with them to make sure they're getting the hang of it. Once they've got it, you'll repeat the process with the second lesson, and then the third, and so on, until you've worked your way through your one-page outline. You may very well find that you need to modify that outline as you go, and that's perfectly fine—this is the part where investing more time and energy to make sure your students are happy and successful is absolutely worthwhile.

Many course creators approach this part of the process thinking that it's about the technology of delivery, or the handouts or worksheets or exercises—but none of that is true. In fact, you'll want to keep the technological complexity to an absolute minimum. Depending on the nature and subject matter of your pilot, and the number of students that you enroll, you can deliver your course through a simple video-conferencing technology like Skype or Zoom. You'll definitely want to deliver the material live, though—prerecorded videos are not only unnecessary at this stage, but they're also counterproductive, as you can't get real-time feedback from students who watch videos the way you can when you're delivering the training to them live. It might not be as pretty or polished as your finished course will one day be, precisely because it will be more raw, more authentic, and geared to be adaptable to what your students need in the moment. That level of intimacy will create a powerful bond between you and your students, a great experience for them, and the best opportunities for you to see what's working and what isn't so that you can evolve and adapt on the fly. If all your students are in your geographic region, you can even deliver the pilot in person. The more opportunities you have to see your students' faces and hear their questions as you work through the material, the better.

Delivering your pilot will be a whirlwind experience with its fair share of ups and downs. Expect it to be exhilarating at times and challenging at others. As long as you plan for that to happen, schedule time in your calendar to deal with all the questions and complications that you don't yet see coming, remain open to evolving your curriculum in response to the reaction of your students, and keep their successful outcomes as your top priority, everything will be fine. Within a few weeks or months of starting, your pilot course will be done, and the time will have come to make an important decision: what should you do next?

STEP 6: PIVOT, ITERATE, OR SCALE

It's been a long and winding road, and you've finally made it to the other side! You've chosen the topic of your pilot, narrowed it down to a minimum viable outcome, and created your one-page plan. You reached out to likely prospects and enrolled some of them in your pilot. And then the real work began, with the delivery of your ideas. The process was exciting and exhilarating, with both ups and downs. But now it's done. The pilot has been delivered, and it's time to take stock and decide what you should do next. There are three dimensions on which you'll want to evaluate the pilot:

1. STUDENT OUTCOMES. Before they signed up for the pilot, you made promises about the outcomes that your students could look forward to. How has that played out? Are your students happy and satisfied? Are you proud to tell others about their outcomes?

2. FINANCIAL PERFORMANCE. Did you make as much money as you had hoped with the pilot? Was it financially successful

beyond your wildest dreams? Did it just meet your expectations? Or was it a disappointment?

3. YOUR EXPERIENCE. At the end of the day, it's very important for you to enjoy your work. So did you enjoy the experience of delivering your pilot? Was it more fun than you ever expected? Was it stressful and frustrating?

Now, in evaluating your pilot, remember that your first attempt at anything is bound to be messy—that's exactly why we pilot rather than build out a full course from scratch. It stands to reason, then, that the results of your pilot on these three dimensions are likely to be mixed: not terrible, but not always amazing, either. And that's perfectly fine, because you don't want to evaluate the pilot based on how it went, but rather on how it would go the next time, informed by what you've learned.

In other words, knowing what you now do, how would it go if you did it again? Do you feel confident that the next time you deliver this training it will be a smashing success on all fronts? Do you have ideas about how to make it great that still need to be validated? Or was the experience such that the biggest takeaway was to never ever try that again? That is unlikely, but much better for you to learn that sooner rather than later!

The relatively rare worst-case scenario is that you will have learned that this is not the path for you to take, so your next step should be to pivot to a new idea. Go back to the drawing board, find a new topic and direction, and start over. And while you're at it, celebrate that it took you only a few months to learn this, rather than the years that it takes so many entrepreneurs!

Sometimes, you'll find that you have an idea of how to make it great, but you need to validate it to be sure. In that case, your next step is to deliver a second pilot course. Change everything that you think needs to be changed, validate your assumptions, and go from there.

And often, you will have learned enough from the pilot that you are now confident in your abilities to deliver an excellent course to a larger number of students. This is the ultimate winning scenario, because it lays a real foundation for you to create leverage, freedom, and impact by teaching your gift.

Chapter 4

HOW TO ATTRACT PAYING STUDENTS

"Content is the party. Promotion is the invitation to attend."

-Nathan Ellering

THERE IS SOMETHING DEEPLY SPECIAL about the moment of sale in an online course business. For the students, it is the crystallization of a decision that the knowledge and skills on offer are more valuable than the dollars they will trade to obtain them, and a symbol of their commitment (however fleeting it might be) to do their part along the way. And for the course creator, it is a powerful shift from the promises of what you will deliver to the reality of what you must.

That moment of sale is critical, but also mysterious, to many course entrepreneurs. Where will you find those interested strangers who are eager to learn what you have to teach? How will you convince them to part with their hard-earned cash? What tactics are aligned with your ethics and brand, and how do you feel about the act of sales as a whole? Marketing and sales are uncomfortable spheres for many experts who dream of creating courses, yet they must learn to navigate those arenas, because one thing is certain: until somebody buys something, all you have on your hands is an idea or project. And until you have a way of attracting leads and customers that is scalable, sustainable, and profitable, you don't have a real business.

And it's not as (unreasonably) easy as it was in the early days, that's for certain. Back then you could create any old web page or write any half-decent ad and open the floodgates to a massive amount of cheap or free leads that were untouched by the vagaries of the online business world. Those days are long gone, though, except for holdovers in a few obscure pockets of the internet, or the businesses of a few legacy successes where reality has not quite caught up yet. But even in those cases, it's a bit like Wile E. Coyote running off a cliff—it might take a moment for gravity to catch up with them, but that doesn't mean they're safe where they stand!

What follows is an exploration of the tried-and-true approaches that work consistently for the coaches, consultants, speakers, authors, and experts that I've trained over the past decade. Their experience (and mine) tells us that the strategy that will attract the paying students you seek will vary depending on the specifics of your business, and especially the stage of the course business journey that you're on. So let's begin at the beginning, with the co-creation of your first pilot course. We've already explored the logic behind the approach in Chapter 3, but now let's turn our attention to the mechanics of actually doing it.

THE MECHANICS OF CO-CREATION

The question on the table is, how do you actually enroll paying students in your pilot course before you've even built it? And how do you do it without turning into a pushy salesperson or giving your nearest and dearest the impression that you've just joined some sort of network marketing fad? There are two answers to this question: the one that a lot of people want to hear, and the real one.

The wished-for answer is one that offers a process that doesn't cost much or any money, reaches an infinite quantity of prospective students, and convinces them to sign up and pay you money without you ever having to do anything uncomfortable like get on the phone and talk to them. Essentially, it's a magical internet "easy button," the idea that if you hit on just the right strategy with just the right technologies and platforms, internet riches will be yours. Obviously, there's no such button that I can offer you—but you already knew that, right?

The real answer involves stepping beyond your comfort zone and doing things that are sometimes uncomfortable. You'll have to walk before you run; start with people who already like and trust you before reaching out to strangers. And actually talk to people so that you can learn what language and ideas they respond to the best, and get feedback as to why they might not be responding at all. The process that I'll lay out won't sound sexy the way that some hit-or-miss "viral social media" strategy might, but it will have the benefit of actually working (I've seen it happen for thousands of course creators). And it will create a foundation for larger successes that will follow.

Let's dive in, starting with being very clear about the scope of what we want to accomplish: The goal right now isn't to attract hundreds or thousands (or hundreds of thousands!) of students to your course. That will happen eventually, but you aren't there yet. Right now the goal is to attract anywhere from a handful to a few dozen students to your pilot course. With them, you can validate that the direction you've chosen is valuable enough to your market that students are happy to pay for it. And you can co-create the experience with them to confirm that you can deliver on your promises.

Over time, as you seek to enroll an ever-growing number of students, the tools, platforms, and strategies that you'll use to find them will grow in number and complexity. But to attract and enroll your pilot students, things are simpler. The specific tools, technologies, and messages that you'll use may vary depending on the industry that you're in and the resources and expertise that you bring to bear. But it will always boil down to reaching out to people you already have some sort of connection with, either personally or professionally, and telling them about it.

Yes, that's right. Your first customers should be people you are already connected with, not strangers on the internet who discover you through ads, blogs, partner referrals, social media, or some other happy accident of browsing the web. There are two reasons for this:

1. THEY ALREADY LIKE AND TRUST YOU. Selling anything can be difficult, and selling something for the first time can be especially challenging, because you probably haven't quite figured out what the most compelling parts are of your promise or nailed the best way of presenting it. Given all that, it makes sense to start with an audience that is friendly and at least somewhat on your side.

2. YOU ALREADY HAVE ACCESS TO THEM. This is very important; you're already going to have to step out of your comfort zone to do this, but why make things harder than they have to be? The broad topic that you chose for your pilot course is of interest to people that you already have access to, isn't it? If so, then this is by far the easiest way of getting started. And if not, you might want to reconsider the topic of your first course.

Of course, your personal and professional networks aren't an eternally renewable resource; you can't keep going back to find more and more customers, and special care must be taken to preserve the relationships that you've worked so hard to build—hence the need for a carefully crafted process.

HOW TO APPROACH PEOPLE YOU KNOW

The first step in approaching people you know is to make a list of the people who are likely to be interested in the subject matter that you're looking to teach, and more specifically in the outcome that you intend to deliver to them. This isn't about cold-calling everyone you've ever met; the only people you should even approach with this are the ones you think could very plausibly find it interesting.

Remember, this is a co-creation process, so you aren't going to call them up and give them a hard sell on paying for your pilot course, like some used-car salesman! Rather, start by reaching out (through whatever channel is most comfortable for you, whether that means email, Facebook, text message, phone, or something else) and sharing that you're starting to work on a new project that you'd love to run by them and get their perspective on. Ask if they can make the time for a quick phone call in the next couple of weeks. You might worry that your contacts will be busy, or uncomfortable accepting a call, but my experience is that people are usually surprised by how well and how quickly this works.

It works because it's actually a pretty innocuous request. If you reach out to a few dozen people, you're likely to be on the phone with many of them in short order. On those calls, you'll simply share the honest truth, which is that you're thinking about teaching a course about your chosen subject matter. Based on whatever background your contacts have that led you to believe they might be interested, indicate that you wanted to reach out and get their input on whether they think this sounds like a course that someone might be interested in signing up for. And ask if it, perhaps, is a course that they themselves might like to sign up for.

The beauty of this question is that at this stage, it is purely hypothetical. If it isn't at all appealing to them, they can say no, which is a gift to you because it means you'll have learned early that the market might not want this course quite as much as you had thought. If that's what they say, ask them to elaborate on their reasons, emphasizing that you aren't trying to change their minds, but rather just wanting to understand; after all, you'd hate to go ahead with this plan if there isn't a demand for it!

But most people won't say no so soon in the conversation, if only because they want to be polite. This is a good thing, because even if they tell you they're not interested later, you want that decision to be as well informed as possible so you can learn from it. This brings us to the other possible answer that they can give you, which is "maybe." That's as good as it gets at this stage, because you haven't really given them enough information to make any stronger of a commitment.

So if they do say "maybe," you can share more information about your pilot course, including what you plan on teaching, what the outcomes will be, what a full-priced course might eventually cost, whether you intend to offer a discount to your pilot students in exchange for their feedback through the process, and when the pilot is going to start. Having shared all that, you're now ready to ask the pivotal question: "Would you like a spot in the pilot?"

There are now three possible answers to this question. The best answer for you, of course, is a yes, in which case you can arrange payment logistics, and you're off to the races. The next-best answer is a no; you haven't enrolled a student, but you've still gotten a clear decision. Just as before, you'll want to press for more details as to why, emphasizing that you aren't trying to convince them, just trying to understand. The worst answer you can get is some variation of "maybe" ("I might," "I'm not sure," "I have to talk to my spouse," etc.). In that case, just ask them to arrive at a decision one way or the other by a certain date (e.g. "next Friday"), so that you know where you stand. And if they don't make a decision by that time, you can treat it as a no. Remember that the goal here isn't to aggressively push for a sale, but rather for you to gain clarity as to why they aren't interested.

If your pilot idea doesn't have legs, then a couple dozen calls is all that you'll have invested before being able to pivot to a new idea that stands to be more valuable for others, and more lucrative for you. And if it does have legs, then a couple dozen phone calls should be all that it takes to fill your inaugural class with paying students. Now, again, I'll emphasize that the goal here isn't to enroll hundreds of students; anywhere from a handful to a few dozen is plenty. So suspend disbelief, take a deep breath, and try it—if you're like many of my students, you'll find that the process is easier, more effective, and maybe even more fun than you're expecting.

ASSEMBLING A SCALABLE MARKETING MACHINE

Approaching people who already like and trust you and engaging in a process of co-creation gives you an edge at a time when you need it most. That said, your personal network isn't exactly a renewable source of leads. Once you've made the rounds, you have to wait awhile before doing it again, and there's a low ceiling on how many times you can go back before people rightly wonder if you like them for anything other than their potential buying power. So once you have the proof of concept, initial validation, and case studies afforded by your first batches of pilot students, it's time to build a more scalable and profitable marketing engine for your online course business.

And that's the name of the game at this stage: scalability. It means that whatever action you take to find leads and convert sales could conceivably be done many more times without hitting limits of supply. It doesn't mean that it is necessarily feasible for you to actually do it many more times in the way that you're doing it, but it means that the supply is available if you could. So, for example, reaching out to your personal networks is not scalable, because of that low ceiling on how many people most of us know. On the other hand, running ads on Facebook or attending local networking events (assuming you live in a major metro area) are both scalable, because you can do as much of them as you want. You don't actually have the bandwidth or resources to do so—your Facebook ads will be constrained by the money you have to spend, and your networking activities will be constrained by the hours in your day. But there's a vast supply of opportunity for you to tap, once you find a way of doing it.

And an important part of scalability is profitability, meaning that if you figure in all the costs of attracting and enrolling the students, you're still profitable. And note that when I say all the costs, I mean *all* the costs: both hard costs that cost exact numbers of dollars that are easily counted (like paying for Facebook ads, where the amount you spend to acquire a customer has to be a fraction of what you'll earn when they buy your course) and also soft costs, which most entrepreneurs tend to devalue (like the time you might spend attending networking events). The calculation of hours that it takes to do the networking, multiplied by the rate of someone you would hire to do that networking for you has to add up to less than you'll earn on your course sales. (For a refresher on unit economics and profitability, refer back to Chapter 2.)

Now, I know what you might be thinking: "Networking? Scale limits? This all sounds very labor-intensive! I thought I was going to learn about marketing wizardry that allows me to sell to strangers on autopilot!" Well, you're not wrong—eventually, that's what we're aiming for. But we can't jump straight to that from selling our first few dozen pilots. Before we can create that level of automation and freedom, we need a scalable and profitable system that works. And that system will fundamentally involve two parts: first, a way of finding and attracting the right strangers, and then a way of turning those strangers into paying students.

WHERE TO FIND THE RIGHT STRANGERS (ATTRACTING LEADS)

Attracting the right strangers starts with a picture of the perfect stranger that you want to attract. Maybe you already know exactly who that is because they were one of your pilot students. Or maybe your pilot students weren't quite the right fit, and you have a hypothesis about what a better ideal student would look like. There's no "right answer" to this question, only a "best answer at the moment"—and that best answer informs where you start looking for more of those ideal students.

Once you have that picture in your mind, you can create an imagined schedule of their day, week, month, and year. In each of those cycles of time, what you're looking for are the places where they might be reached by someone seeking to influence them with a helpful educational message. Here are some of the places you might look:

- DAILY/WEEKLY: Where do they live? Where do they work? What apps do they use? What websites do they visit? What social networks are they active on? What publications do they read? What podcasts do they listen to?

- WEEKLY/MONTHLY: What classes do they take? What activities do they participate in? What events do they attend? What influencers do they follow? What books do they read? What trainings do they take? What speakers do they listen to?

- MONTHLY/YEARLY: Where do they travel? What conferences do they attend? What training do they invest in? What brands do they engage with?

Any number of possible places to reach your ideal stranger might emerge from this exploration: from business networking to public speaking, from social networks to online search, from industry conferences to print publications, and everything in between. Create your list of possible places, without worrying just yet about feasibility or likelihood of success.

Now, the thing about attracting strangers is that it's not just about knowing where they are—you also have to get their attention. So for each of those possible places to intercept them, you'll want to explore what the mechanism would be that would attract enough of their attention to get on their radar. Is it as simple as a conversation and business card? Will you have to lead a breakout session or presentation? Is a free e-book the way to get noticed?

In answering these questions, remember that you're not actually looking for answers so much as educated guesses, because unless you've already done exactly what you're looking to do (in which case it isn't speculative, and you probably don't need this section of the book to help you), this is uncharted territory for you. You're in hypothesis-testing mode, just as you were in the piloting stage with regard to other assumptions about your course business.

The key is to start designing experiments: If you think the people you're looking for will be found at conferences, how might you test that assumption? Which conferences might you attend, how might you need to show up, and what might you need to prepare to see whether you're on the right track? (Replace *conferences* with *social media ads* or *networking* or *speaking* or *SEO* or whatever strategy might seem to best fit your situation and market.)

You'll want to execute those experiments, with the expectation that—just like your pilot, or anything else that you try for the first time—you probably won't knock it out of the park initially. So don't make your first attempt a Hail Mary pass; to paraphrase business guru Jim Collins, use bullets first, and cannonballs after you've validated that you're pointing at the right target. And remember that you're not just testing the *where* of reaching your target stranger; you're also testing the *how* of converting them to students.

HOW TO TURN STRANGERS INTO STUDENTS (CONVERTING SALES)

Nobody wakes up in the morning, rolls out of bed, and thinks to themselves that today is a good day to spend thousands of dollars on something they don't even know exists yet. Resources are scarce, and we're all legitimately guarded and cautious about where we choose to invest them. So before getting to a place where they're ready to invest a substantial amount of time, money, and energy in anything, there are things that your future student needs to know, understand, and believe—about the broader opportunity in which you operate, about themselves, and of course about you and your course.

ABOUT THE OPPORTUNITY. Before anything else, people need to believe that the problem they're looking to solve is actually solvable. This may seem obvious, but unless people are actively looking for a solution, it can't be taken as a given. More often, when people have persistent problems it means those problems have dropped from the top of their priorities (downgraded from acute to chronic). In that scenario, some part of them has given up on the idea of the problem actually being solvable, and they've externalized responsibility as to why that is the case: relationships don't work because of the people around them, they can't get on top of their finances because the system is rigged against them, and they're stuck with their weight because of their genes. In all cases, they find a rationalization for why it's not their fault and why there's nothing they can do about it. That being the case, before they can even entertain the idea of buying a course to solve a problem, they need to be open to the possibility of the problem being solvable. This takes a shift in worldview, and it is the first thing that you as course entrepreneur need to impart.

ABOUT THEMSELVES. Disbelief comes in waves. The first is about the problem: They may say, "No, it can't be solved; this is just how it is." Once you dispel that, there's a new defense to overcome if they say, "Okay, yes, I see how this can work for some people (out there, in the world), but that doesn't mean it will work for me. Because I'm different. I'm special." This is where you need to show that not just is the problem solvable for people in general, but also specifically for people just like the ideal student you're trying to attract: someone in their situation, with their same circumstances, challenges, and peculiarities. It's only after you show them definitively that a solution is eminently available to people just like them that they are ready to learn about you and your course.

ABOUT YOU AND YOUR COURSE. Once they're ready to learn about the specific thing that you're offering, there's a lot that they want to know: What does it include? How does it work? How long does it last? What will you cover? What does it cost? What results do you guarantee? These are just a few of the many, many questions that they'll ask. But behind all these questions, there are three broad categories of things that they really need to understand: relevancy, credibility, and urgency:

- RELEVANCY ("WHY THIS?")—How does your course address the opportunity that they face and the need that they experience? Why is it the best option for getting what they want?

- CREDIBILITY ("WHY YOU?")—What makes you the most trustworthy vendor to learn from? What about your credentials, case studies, and the guarantees will make them feel most comfortable?

- URGENCY ("WHY NOW?")—Why do they need to do this now, rather than at some point in the future? What is the reason for acting now, today, before other priorities obscure their view?

In some cases, especially if you're selling an inexpensive course about a super-desirable topic to an audience of innovators and early adopters, the list of things you need to convey is relatively short and lends itself to a simple and straightforward process. Other times, more commonly when dealing with premium transformative courses sold to mainstream buyers, it takes a little more heavy lifting to get the job done.

Now, with some clarity about what needs to be conveyed, you can start thinking about which mechanisms will be best suited to get those points across. Will a simple email sequence do the trick? Do you need an elaborate sales letter or video? Will you send direct physical mail? Or will you perhaps offer a webinar, participatory bootcamp, in-person event, or interaction with a salesperson?

Again, you'll be dealing in the realm of hypotheses and testing, and none of the things you try are likely to work perfectly right off the bat. But you'll find the mechanisms that work more effectively than others and then slowly work to improve them through subsequent iterations. That's the first step toward applying automation and acceleration, which we'll explore in just a moment. But first, a word is needed about how this process works in the context of the complex sales cycles in business-to-business environments.

HOW TO THINK ABOUT B2B AND OTHER COMPLEX SALES CYCLES

Of the thousands upon thousands of coaches, consultants, speakers, authors, and experts that my organization has trained to build and sell courses, about a third operates in business-to-business (B2B) environments, meaning that they sell their courses into organizations. And while it's true that fundamentally every buyer is a person, there are differences in process and experience when you're selling to an organization with complex approval processes, multiple stakeholders to get on board, and specific budgetary criteria that need to be met.

But that is not to say that it can't be done, or even that it is particularly difficult. But it is *different*, and if you try to apply the same processes as you would in a business-to-consumer environment, it isn't likely to work very well. The key to navigating these differences is to understand the difference between a buying *modality* and a buying *process*.

Buying modalities are primarily about the medium that moves someone from "Contemplation" to "Action"—for example, reading a sales letter, watching a sales presentation, or talking to a salesperson. The reason why online marketing can be so effective is that it is fairly easy to substitute one medium with another; for example, the printed sales letter can become a web page, the sales presentation can become a webinar or video, and the salesperson can work just as effectively over the phone or video conference, and can even be augmented by artificial intelligence through tools like Facebook Messenger bots.

Buying processes, on the other hand, are about the steps and stakeholders involved in reaching a sale. For example, the line manager, HR director, and VP of finance might all need to sign off on a sale, and it might have to go through two rounds of budgetary approval. Whereas there is a great deal of room to experiment with different buying modalities, the buying process itself is a lot harder to change, and attempts to circumvent the stakeholders and cycles are likely to end in failure. (Imagine telling a line manager that they don't need their bosses to be on board and have to skip the approval cycles, because the doors are closing tomorrow—that isn't likely to be effective!)

So if you're selling into a corporate environment (or any environment with a complex buying process), don't let the allure of automated internet marketing seduce you away from serving the people who need to be on board as they take the steps that they have to traverse. Remember that what you're ultimately solving for at this stage in the game is scalability, which means that if you had unlimited time and resources, you could apply this same process to as many organizations as you would want, and that on the basis of dollars and hours invested to make the sale, it would be profitable with each and every one. As long as these are both true, you'll be well positioned to accelerate the process once it's working.

ACCELERATING YOUR MARKETING FLYWHEEL

The co-creation process is great for enrolling your first few dozen students, and the experimentation with lead sources and conversion mechanisms will bring in your next few hundred. Once you've passed those stages, you have everything you need to build the system that attracts the next several thousand students (and more), with less and less effort on your part. This is the acceleration of your marketing flywheel—the holy grail that course entrepreneurs dream about creating.

The first step is a process that works to scalably find the right strangers and convert them to customers. And remember our definition of *scalability*: It's not that effort isn't required, but rather that the effort (time, money, energy) that you put in is more than justified by the profit you get out, and that the opportunity is large enough for you to do as much of it as you'd like. Once that process is in place, you can start streamlining and scaling it, through systems and delegation:

SYSTEMS. To some extent, building systems will happen naturally; the first time you do anything is messy and inefficient, but by the tenth time, you'll know at least some of the best practices, have templates for repeated steps, and know the blind alleys to avoid. Whether your chosen strategy involves networking events, Facebook ads, speaking on stages, or engaging in joint ventures, there are specific steps to follow along the path, and you'll have templates that you can use to complete those steps faster. You'll also start plugging holes—for example, the exact places in the process where meeting planners and partners are likely to go dark, or when ad costs are likely to start rising. You'll develop specific action steps to minimize the risks and take advantage of hidden opportunities. And as you build these systems into your process, you'll find that with each successive run-through you exert less effort and get better results. That creates added profitability, which you can apply toward delegation.

DELEGATION. Some marketing strategies are only moderately time-consuming, whereas others are extremely so, as with activities like networking, speaking, or face-to-face sales. That's not a problem, though, as long as all the time and energy invested are properly accounted for in your profit margins. Once the process is properly streamlined, you can start handing off the responsibilities to others on your team, starting with the small stuff and then gradually getting to the areas of higher leverage. A networking strategy, for example, can be augmented by an assistant who can do a lot of the follow-ups for you, and then eventually it can be taken over completely by a salesperson on your payroll. The same goes for any strategy that you might apply—as long as the unit economics work and the systems are effective, you can gradually come to delegate more and more of the process to allow for ever greater scale.

The beauty of this sort of acceleration is that momentum begets momentum, and success begets success. The first turns on that flywheel are always a struggle, but the more it spins, the easier it gets, and the more efficiencies and resources you have to apply toward making it spin even faster. Will it take a few years to go from winning idea to profitable flywheel? Sure, but you can do well for yourself along the way, and if you see the process all the way through, then you're really living the dream.

Important note: I realize that, especially with regard to the more advanced stages of marketing, this chapter has focused on higher-level generalities. This is by necessity, because the details will depend entirely on the strategies that make sense for your business; entire books have been written on specific strategies like speaking, running ads, and everything in between. That said, my organization does provide additional resources about specific strategies. To explore them, feel free to take advantage of the invitations on the next page.

ADDITIONAL RESOURCES TO SUPPORT YOU!

GET THE AUDIOBOOK + COURSE BUSINESS TOOL KIT

Receive the free audiobook PLUS our Course Business Tool Kit, which contains valuable downloads and worksheets to help you create your own online course business.

→ Download it at **TeachYour.Gift/toolkit**

PARTICIPATE IN THE COURSE BUILDER'S BOOTCAMP

Ready to start your own online course business journey? Our weeklong intensive Course Builder's Bootcamp is a crash course in everything you need to get started.

→ Sign up for free at **TeachYour.Gift/bootcamp**

JOIN US IN PERSON AT TEACH YOUR GIFT LIVE

Receive best-in-class training, discover cutting-edge strategies, and connect with a community of your fellow coach, consultant, author, speaker, and expert course entrepreneurs.

→ Reserve your spot at **TeachYour.Gift/live**

Chapter 5

CREATING A WORLD-CLASS COURSE

"Education is not the learning of facts,
but the training of a mind to think."

-ALBERT EINSTEIN

IN 2013, Jane (not her real name) was a frustrated artist, stuck in the same place as many creatives and artists: doing what she loved (participating in exhibitions and mentoring other artists), but not making a living. Her day job paid the bills, but it left limited time for the creative work that excited her. She loved teaching other people to improve their art, but there were only so many students she could find in her local area, and only so much she could charge for a class or retreat. She wasn't getting any closer to making a living from her creative expertise.

She decided to look into taking her work online so she could reach more people and develop a new revenue stream. Like many new businesses, she started small. She launched her first online course and enrolled nine students. Total revenue? Less than a thousand dollars.

Yet this first small step was the beginning of a multiyear journey that would lead Jane to develop new ways of teaching art online, serve thousands of students, and ultimately support herself entirely through teaching and mentoring.

Jane was able to achieve so much because of the positive feedback loop that exists in successful course businesses—building momentum and increasing the payoff of incremental effort. It's hard to get it started, but once it's there, it's powerful. It starts with your first course and first students. This isn't glamorous; it's often a manual process that takes time and effort. But it is a big step forward to go from zero to one, from never having had a course or students before to being up and running.

That's the first step: getting customers. But just getting that first small group of customers isn't worth much on its own. It's rarely enough to make your business sustainable. The next step is to get your customers *results*, so they're incredibly happy with your course. Your course has to *work*. It needs to help your learners achieve the outcomes or transformation they care about. A course on stress reduction should help people feel less stressed. A course on hiring great employees should ultimately result in the business owners being happier with their hiring process and the quality of new hires.

Jane invested the time and effort to design art courses that were genuinely different from generic low-cost courses already on the market, with a clear focus on helping participants improve the quality and creativity of their work. Doing this—turning customers into "result getters"—means they'll share their great experience with friends, family, and colleagues (or the entire internet via social media)! Your result getters turn into word spreaders, and that's how your business and profit begin to grow in a healthy and consistent way. The feedback loop is building momentum!

The key to building this cycle is to create a genuinely learner-centered course that leads to positive outcomes for your participants. There are many people with great expertise in high-value areas who try to rest on their laurels; they think they can do a brain dump of all their valuable knowledge, and people will happily pay for it. That approach may lead to a few quick sales, but it will never power the sort of feedback loop that leads to sustained course business success, because students won't be thrilled with their results. That means no referrals, no feedback loop, and no growth over time.

CAN ONLINE COURSES BE TRULY GREAT?

When I teach about creating truly excellent online courses, there's a question lurking in the back of people's minds that is eventually given voice: "Sure, we can make the best of the format, but can an online course ever be as good as the 'real thing'? Is it even possible for it to be more than a poor man's classroom?" The answer is a resounding yes. In fact, online courses have the potential to be dramatically more effective and impactful than their in-person alternatives, but not if we start with an in-person learning experience as the paradigm that we try to model.

In-person learning experiences often leave much to be desired; as famed neuroscientist Dr. John Medina, author of *Brain Rules*, put it: "If you wanted to create an education environment that was directly opposed to what the brain was good at doing, you probably would design something like a classroom." But in-person learning also has redeeming characteristics, created by the convergence of students and teacher at a single place and time. This allows them to connect and learn from each other, which can be highly valuable.

Unfortunately, those benefits don't translate well to an online setting. So as long as a conventional classroom remains our frame of reference, online education will never be more than a "poor man's version" of a real-world classroom. And most of us don't realize just how much that conventional classroom constrains our thinking as to what education can be. We've internalized a long list of assumptions so strongly that it doesn't even occur to us that there are other options. For example, here are some assumptions about the optimal classroom:

- STUDENT-TO-TEACHER RATIO (twenty-five students to one teacher)
- DISTRIBUTION OF SKILL LEVELS OF STUDENTS (all students at the same level)
- LENGTH OF A LESSON OR LESSON SEGMENT (forty-five minutes to one hour per session)
- PACE OF CONTENT DELIVERY (one lesson per week)
- MODALITY FOR CONTENT DELIVERY (lecture style for the whole class)
- WAY TO KEEP STUDENTS MOTIVATED (rewards and punishments)
- WAY TO EVALUATE PROGRESS AND PERFORMANCE (tests and grades)

And that's just the beginning. Most of us have firm implicit assumptions about this topic, which are a reflection of our own experiences in educational settings like elementary, secondary, undergraduate, and graduate classrooms. You might be surprised, then, to know that almost all of those assumptions are incorrect (or at least, incorrect for a large portion of students); in some cases, the jury's still out, and in many other cases, the research has shown conclusively that the way things are conventionally done is appallingly ineffective. But where did all these assumptions come from? Nobody actually set out to create a learning environment that prevents us from learning, so why does education look the way that it does?

The answer is a combination of inertia and the economics that govern an in-person classroom; much of what we do started as somebody's best guess, and it's hard to move past that original best guess when practicality and affordability aren't on your side. Case in point: Many North American educational settings implicitly assume that a single teacher can handle up to twenty-five students. This is based on a determination made by the Jewish scholar Maimonides in the 12th century (who, incidentally, taught students in an oral tradition of chanting Torah and engaging in Talmudic studies—not a typical classroom even in the 12th century!). Since then, many scholars of education have made evidence-based arguments for class sizes of eight to twelve, but still we stick with Maimonides, largely because of the cost and supply of good teachers.

We may roll our eyes at this sort of inertia, but the constraints are real. Even if we know that students would benefit from twice as many qualified teachers than they currently have, that doesn't mean those teachers are available for hire, nor that the money is available to pay them. Research may show that students learn best working at their own pace, but if all the students and teachers have to show up for a lesson to be delivered, there's no choice but to have them all progress as a cohort rather than as individuals. Hands-on interaction with the subject matter might best help us learn, but if that requires access to rare, expensive, or easily damaged equipment, it just isn't practical.

In other words, there are a lot of reasons why most traditional classrooms work the way that they do; some are accidents of history and some are necessities of practicality. That they constrain the future and potential of an entire generation is a tragedy, but that they constrain our imagination as to what education could even look like is a travesty. That's why we must recognize these preconceptions for what they are, set them aside, and reimagine from the ground up what education can be.

HOW MIGHT LEARNING BE REIMAGINED?

There are myriad ways to reimagine the learning process and do better for our students. They are made possible by the fast-evolving technologies of education delivery, the resourcefulness of enterprising teachers, the increased participation and engagement of students, and the borrowing of best practices from other industries. Taken together, these factors more than level the playing field between traditional education institutions and independent education entrepreneurs like you. Here are just a few ideas to whet your appetite and excite your imagination:

- COURSES NO LONGER have to be created first and then sold later. The technology that allows for rapid deployment of new content in real-time means that you can develop a curriculum on the fly with the input of your students to make sure what you're building is exactly aligned with what they want and need.

This can be done through live content delivery or through real-time surveying and adaptation, and as we've already discussed, the counterintuitive outcome of this on-the-fly development is typically a much better learning experience for the student.

- IN THE PAST, curricula had to follow a linear one-size-fits-all path from one lesson to the next, simply because that's the only way for it to unfold when a professor delivers a lecture every week. But now that content can be delivered digitally and virtually, lessons can be laid out in more of a "choose-your-own-adventure" conditional flowchart pattern: If students already know about the first lesson, they can skip it and choose one of the following lessons based on their circumstances. These paths can be predetermined, or they can be chosen and adjusted in real time based on a student's comfort level with whatever they happen to be learning in the moment.

- IF BOTH TEACHER AND STUDENTS must converge at the same place and time for a lecture to be delivered, all parties need to be able to plan for arrival and departure, hence the fixed standard length of a lesson. But the reality is that some content needs longer treatment, and some needs much shorter, which is possible when students and teacher can be untethered from each other. Just as hour-long cable television shows actually run only about forty-two minutes (an hour minus commercials) while Netflix original episodes can be whatever length the content and story calls for, so too will education get better as the constraints of arbitrary lesson lengths become irrelevant.

- TECHNOLOGY-BASED DELIVERY OF CONTENT means that rather than dripping a course out to all participants on an approximation of the average student's best schedule, students can progress at their own pace by "gating" the delivery of new content based on demonstrated understanding of what has already been delivered. This is called *mastery learning* in education circles, and it is responsible for the first standard deviation jump in results for Benjamin Bloom's research participants, which will be discussed later in this chapter. Technology has also made it practical to deliver at scale.

- IN THE WISE WORDS sometimes credited to Benjamin Franklin, "Tell me and I forget, teach me and I may remember, involve me and I will learn." One of the best ways to involve someone in the content is by having them teach it and evaluate the work of others. Creative use of peer grading systems in which students give each other feedback is not only a great way of improving the internalization of the subject matter, but also a great way of scaling the delivery of meaningful feedback to all students. While some educators worry that peer grading is just a matter of the blind leading the blind, research has shown that when implemented correctly, the feedback is just as accurate and helpful as what the teacher would provide, and the process of giving that feedback becomes one of the most valuable parts of the learning process.

- GAMIFICATION TECHNOLOGIES are still in their infancy, but already there are fascinating opportunities for integrating a mix of tracking, feedback, community, and incentives into educational experiences that make the learning process more engaging and experiential, leading to higher levels of educational content consumption and internalization, which in turns leads to higher student completion and success rates.

As you can see, the motivated entrepreneurial educator's palette of possibilities is almost endless (for more ideas and inspiration, visit www.ted.com/playlists/24/re_imagining_school). And just as with any palette, the key isn't to use every color with every brushstroke, but rather to use the right ones in just the right places, for maximum effect, because ultimately, the goal isn't to use every shiny new learning strategy we can find, but rather to make the learning experience truly great.

MOMENTUM VS. FRICTION

Newton's first law of motion states that an object will remain in motion unless acted upon by an external force. In space, that means a little push is all it takes to get you clear across the galaxy, as long as you have enough time and don't bump into anything along the way. Down here on Earth, though, there are lots of external forces such as air pressure, gravity, and friction. As a result, no matter how hard you throw a ball, it will go only so far before slowing and crashing.

Learners' journeys through any educational experience work in much the same way. They set out with a certain amount of momentum, and that momentum is gradually eroded by friction and distraction. If the friction or distraction becomes greater than the momentum forward, they will stop dead in their tracks. Game over. As course creators, our jobs are to plot the course from start to finish (meaning the transformation that comes from the successful application of whatever we're teaching) and find where along the way friction is breaking momentum. With that clarified, we can eliminate friction, add momentum, or do both to keep students moving forward.

This begs the question: What creates friction? Why are so many attics and garages littered with the remnants of unmet goals; the guitar that we never learned to play, the exercise machines that didn't get us in shape, the skis that rode the slopes only three times, the running shoes that never turned into a running habit, and the tools that never made household repairs? Why do we fail to achieve so much of what we set out to achieve? The answer is that in all cases, the challenge is one of changing behavior, and changing behavior is hard. Jonathan Haidt, in his book *The Happiness Hypothesis*, lays out a model for behavior change that spells out the three categories of friction that might get in our way, using the metaphor of a rider on an elephant navigating a path.

The Rider is your rational mind, typified by the prefrontal cortex that looks for patterns, makes plans, predicts the future, monitors the self, and attempts to distinguish between and suppress animal instincts. The rider loves to contemplate and analyze, doing so with a negative bias—almost always focusing on problems rather than solutions. The rider is frustrated by uncertainty and easily exhausted. Removing friction for the rider is all about cognitive load, which is the total amount of mental effort being used in working memory. When cognitive load is high, so is the friction. In other words, if something is confusing your students—whether it's your instructions or your actual lessons—that can create cognitive friction that the students can't handle.

The Elephant is your emotional mind, typified by the amygdala that is the root of fear and trigger of the body's stress response.

Negative emotion has a narrowing effect on range of thought, while positive emotion allows the mind to wander creatively. The elephant is easily spooked and hates doing things with no immediate benefit. It is stubborn, needs reassurance, and is quickly demoralized. It is powerful, tireless, and difficult to actively direct. Removing friction for the elephant is the hardest sort of friction to solve. This is about the stuff that we know how to do and have a clear path to accomplish, but that we don't feel comfortable doing. For example, explaining the mechanics of how to sell is fairly straightforward, and students can memorize a script without much difficulty. But actually navigating a sales conversation and addressing questions of value and affordability is uncomfortable because money can be uncomfortable. We can support students by giving them a chance to gear up for the challenge. Like running a marathon, it's a lot easier to do it if you know what it's going to take and you've prepared.

The Path is the environment, the external stimuli making up the world that the mind consciously and unconsciously interprets and reacts to. Forces such as convenience, distraction, and cognitive biases play a significant role in directing behavior. Even when the rider and the elephant cooperate, they must know in what direction to head. Without a clear vision of the destination, change will not happen, as the elephant tends to follow the path of least resistance. Friction along the path has grown substantially in our current age of technological marvel, where everything we want is a key press or voice command away. To say that this has made us impatient is an enormous understatement, so much so that Amazon's tests show that a page speed slowdown of just one second could cost $1.6 billion in sales each year. As a course creator who slaves over a lesson, I find it frustrating when students abandon it because of the smallest technical challenge, but it's also good news. In the grand scheme of things, fixing user experience challenges is fairly simple. The first step is to audit the students' experience and get a sense of any steps that might create more friction than necessary.

With the clear intention of creating a high-momentum experience with as little friction as possible for the rider and the elephant along the path, we're finally ready to turn our attention to designing the actual course.

SIX LAYERS OF LEARNING

Great chefs know that all dishes and flavors are created by some blend of the presence or absence of five basic tastes: sweet, sour, bitter, salty, and umami (savory). In much the same way, every learning experience is the product of six different components, each layered on top of the next: content, success behaviors, delivery, user experience, accountability, and support. Let's explore each of them in turn.

(Note: What follows is an adaptation of the Six Layers of Learning that are described in much greater detail in Chapter 10 of my 2018 book *Leveraged Learning*, which you're welcome to buy, or read for free at LeveragedLearningBook.com.)

LAYER #1: CONTENT (WHAT WILL BE TAUGHT TO GET STUDENTS WHERE THEY'RE GOING)

As I've emphasized throughout, your course is about so much more than just that content. That said, without content there is no course, so the first step is to define what you need to cover to get your

students the results that you want to promise. And take it further—
it's not just about *what* they need to know; it's also about *how well*
they need to know it.

Once you've got some ideas down, you can explore some tips
and tricks for communicating them in a way that supports people in
their learning. There is an entire field of study devoted to this, called
Instructional Design. I won't try to make you an expert in just a few
pages, but I can share a few tips, which I call the 3 S's of Instructional
Design, as a sort of crash course to help you get a leg up as you get
started: Small Wins, Scaffolding, and Stories.

SMALL WINS are simple milestones in your pilot that give your
students a sense of accomplishment and confidence. They can be
something as simple as filling out your participation contract or understanding a basic topic and speaking up on a weekly call. The idea is
to ask your students to do something, see them do it, and in some way
reinforce their action as a job well done, no matter how simple it is.

Small wins are important because they make your students feel
successful, which helps them gain confidence as they move forward
and tackle more challenging tasks. The key here is pacing. You want
to stretch your students at every step and teach them slightly more
complex information as your pilot progresses, but you also want them
to experience wins along the way. Ideally, you want to incorporate
small wins early in your program so that you create positive energy
that keeps students excited about learning more. Then you can look
for pivot points in your training where students should have mastered a particular skill and are ready to move on to more challenging
concepts. Those pivot points are ideal spots to provide opportunities
for wins. From my experience in different training courses built by
my own company Mirasee, as well as by the thousands of students

we've taught, small wins are easily the single biggest factor in leading students to success.

SCAFFOLDING is about creating a layered learning experience so students continually build on the concepts they already know. Start with what your students already know, because either they came to you with that knowledge or you've already taught it to them in a previous lesson. Beginning with simple concepts, gradually layer in more challenging ideas by providing context and telling students how this new information fits into what they already know. Teach new skills by using explanations, examples, and homework to give more understanding, and let them practice what they just learned. Continue to put your students just outside their existing knowledge level, noting that this zone is constantly moving as students learn new material. Repeat this process until students reach a full understanding of what they're looking to accomplish. Do you see how it all works together? You strategically organize your lessons so students feel like they're on a solid foundation before moving on to something new, but you always push them slightly beyond their current skill level. That said, there's one thing you need to watch out for, and that's moving so fast your students never feel like they've mastered one stage before moving on to the next. That's one of the big reasons piloting is so effective—you get to test out your pacing to make sure it works before creating your full course.

STORIES are all about how narratives influence learning and—more importantly—how we should teach. People are hardwired for stories. It's not just that we like them; research has shown that our love of stories goes beyond any emotional or entertainment value they may give us. Our brains actually look for a coherent narrative structure in every communication we experience, and if it's there, it's easier to understand and retain information. Essentially, we need to see a beginning, middle, and end to any communication, and if we do, it's easier for us to absorb the information and relate it to our own experiences. This is key to understanding how you can structure your lessons for easy learning. Basically, you should always organize information into a beginning (where you introduce new concepts), a middle (where you develop and expand on those concepts), and an end (where you tell students how to use them and what comes next). Whenever possible, introduce or reinforce new or difficult concepts with a story or case study. To sum up, two magic words you should find yourself using over and over again are *for example.*

Finally, you should prune your curriculum mercilessly. In the context of learning, there's no such thing as content that is nice to have. Everything is either critical to the understanding and success of your students or an opportunity for them to become distracted, confused, or overwhelmed. So deliver exactly what needs to be taught to achieve the learning outcomes and nothing more.

LAYER #2: SUCCESS BEHAVIORS (WHAT STUDENTS NEED TO SUCCEED)

At the start of every year, aspirations for a happier, healthier life prompt countless resolutions to start going to the gym. This leads to a rush of gym memberships, but sadly, the majority go unused. The same is true of the success rates of people who set out to quit smoking, learn to play guitar, and complete courses they've signed up for. The reason is simple: It's hard to change behavior. In the words of Stephen Covey, "to know and not to do is really not to know." This poses a double challenge for online course creators: We not only need to design learning experiences that empower students to apply and succeed with whatever we're teaching them, but we also have to design a learning experience that instills the behavior of actually consuming and completing the course!

A course that students don't complete, or one that students do complete but don't implement, is of little value. For that reason, the second layer of the learning experience is the *success behaviors* that will see the student through to the finish line. And while the list of possible success behaviors is almost infinite, we choose the most important ones by thinking through what is most likely to prevent students from consuming what we teach and applying what they learn. Sometimes success behaviors are simple and logistical; for example, instructing students to block time off in their schedules each week to complete the course work is both easy and effective. But sometimes, it can be much more involved.

The key is to think ahead and anticipate the challenges, setbacks, and discouragements that students will encounter. If we know what they are, we can prepare students with an effective response that will keep them moving forward. Peter Gollwitzer's research has shown that this "behavioral preloading" can be surprisingly effective, as recounted by Chip and Dan Heath in their book *Switch*: "When people make advance mental commitments—if X happens, then I will do Y—they are substantially more likely to act in support of their goals than people who lack those mental plans. Someone who has committed to drink less alcohol, for instance, might resolve, 'Whenever a waiter asks if I want a second drink, I'll ask for sparkling water.' And that person is far more likely to turn down the drink than someone else who shares the same goal but has no preloaded plan."

LAYER #3: DELIVERY (HOW LEARNING WILL BE PRESENTED AND SHARED)

Deep learning, real understanding, and the development of competence all involve the active participation of the student in the learning process. That doesn't just happen! It must be intentionally designed into the delivery of the curriculum. Learning, after all, is not a spectator sport—learning happens by talking, writing, thinking, experiencing, and doing.

The third layer of the learning experience is about how you engage your participants, move them to action, and help them make progress toward the criteria you've set out. In a course on stress reduction, for example, are students just watching some videos and nodding along, thinking, "yes, this all sounds nice…"? Or are they actually trying specific techniques to deal with stress, integrating those techniques into their day-to-day lives, and seeing results? The key is to find opportunities for students to practice and apply what you teach them.

If it isn't practical for students to immediately practice what you preach, a great tool in the teacher's toolbox is formative assessment with in-process evaluation of comprehension, learning needs, and progress. Offering this sort of frequent, low-stakes feedback on understanding helps students to consolidate and retain what they're learning. This is supported by the research of John Hattie, whose book *Visible Learning* documents his review of hundreds of meta-analyses of student achievement studies, finding that formative assessment ranks third highest out of eight hundred fifteen factors.

You can implement formative assessment in your program by incorporating a series of small assignments that participants submit to you for review. In an art course, these could be specific, focused exercises. In a business course, they might be particular subprojects, such as creating a landing page or writing a marketing email. The key is that participants are actively learning by doing the work, and receiving regular feedback from you.

LAYER #4: USER EXPERIENCE (HOW STUDENTS WILL NAVIGATE THE LEARNING)

For most of the past few centuries, the experience of education remained pretty much the same: A teacher at the front of a class lectured to a roomful of students. Sure, there was variation in terms of the expertise and visual aids of the teacher, the age and skill of the students, and perhaps the reference materials and note-taking equipment at their disposal. But by and large, the students showed up, listened to the teacher, wrote down their notes, and did some reading and homework, either alone or together with their peers.

However, in the past couple of decades, things have been changing at a dizzying pace. The students may be remaining in a classroom, or sitting at home in front of their computer, or even out jogging and listening through their earbuds. The instructor may be delivering the lesson in real time, or using a recording made weeks or years in advance. Students may meet in person to collaborate, or they may use a telephone, a messaging tool like Slack, or a video conferencing tool such as Skype or Zoom. They may read books and articles, or watch videos, or listen to audio recordings, or even participate in virtual or augmented reality simulations. Students may be digital natives who are fluent in all these technologies, or baby boomers who feel bewildered by it all, or anywhere in between. The same is true of the instructor.

Navigating this landscape is challenging, but it helps to remember that the technology isn't an end in and of itself—it is just a means for getting there. So don't worry too much about everything that might be possible, and focus more on what the very best way is for delivering the experience that you've already designed. Look for technology that facilitates the experience you want to create, and don't worry about the rest.

LAYER #5: ACCOUNTABILITY (THE COMMUNITY AND TRIGGERS TO STAY ON TASK)

On September 5, 2010, I joined roughly 20,000 participants at the starting line of the Oasis Rock 'N' Roll Montreal Marathon. It was a beautiful day, and we were all excited when the starting bell rang. I ran at a brisk pace, enjoyed the fresh air, and high-fived the volunteers at the early mile markers. Then I started to get tired. The distance between racers increased as initially small differences in pace translated to bigger differences in distance and time. I discovered that I hadn't trained nearly as long or hard as I should have, and I was feeling that deficit. But I pushed through, sometimes running, sometimes walking, but always moving forward. Around the twentieth mile, I hit "the wall," the sudden wave of fatigue that sets in toward the end of the race and threatens to crush runners. I barely persevered and limped over the finish line with the thoroughly unimpressive time of about six hours. At many points along the way, I was tempted to quit. The race was long, I was tired, and my legs ached, so quitting would have been easy. Why did I keep on going? Part of the reason was a commitment to myself, part was the context of all the racers around me, and part was the accountability to all my friends who knew I was doing it. I would have to tell them that I had quit, and that was a distinctly unappealing idea. But the most important factor by a wide margin was that I ran the race with my then girlfriend and now wife! This reversed the effect of an insidious challenge to behavior change: hyperbolic discounting.

Hyperbolic discounting essentially means that we give more weight to consequences that are immediate than to consequences that wait for us further in the future. For example, given the choice between ten dollars today and eleven dollars tomorrow, most people choose eleven dollars. Given the choice between ten dollars today and eleven dollars next year, though, most people go for the ten dollars today. It's the logic of "better a bird in the hand than ten on the bush." Hyperbolic discounting is the root of the challenge with doing coursework, training for and running a marathon, and pretty much every other thing that we want to do and know is good for us: The benefits are far off into the future, but the cost is right here, right now. For example, next year I'll be glad that I finished the marathon, but right now I feel like quitting. Tomorrow I'll be glad that I went to bed early, but right now I feel like watching a few more episodes of *Game of Thrones*. As a species, we aren't very good at choosing what we *want* over what we *feel like* in the moment.

Accountability is so important because it reverses the effects of hyperbolic discounting, by adding both pleasure and pain that enforce the immediate decisions we actually want to make. Sure, I was tired and felt like quitting that race, but I was enjoying the company of my peers, and the physical pain in my legs didn't hold a candle to the emotional pain of quitting in front of my girlfriend! Accountability, along with the community that provides it, is among the most important factors that keep us on target while moving toward our goals. Conversely, a lack of accountability and structure is one of the greatest challenges in the transition from mandatory to volitional education; for example, if I can choose to watch lesson materials and do the work on any day of the week, in any week of the year, in any year of the next decade, then the odds that I won't do it at all increase dramatically. This makes it incumbent on course creators to build accountability into our learning experiences. A couple of practical ways to do this are forcing a minimum progression speed and raising the stakes:

- FORCING A MINIMUM PROGRESSION. Sometimes the simplest solution is to take away some of that extra choice. Adding some structure to a program in which everybody starts on a certain date, must meet certain deadlines, and completes the program together can have a dramatic impact on completion rates.

- RAISING THE STAKES. This is implicit in the previous suggestion (such as if missing a deadline has consequences), but can be taken to a whole new level. An extreme example is a commitment contract, described by Ian Ayres in his book *Carrots and Sticks*: committing yourself to donate money to a cause that you despise (an "anti-charity") if you don't meet your commitments.

Accountability is a powerful way to keep students moving forward, but be careful about applying it to compensate for other challenges in your course design. If students are getting stuck because of technology issues (like not being able to find their password or having trouble navigating the course site), the promise of an incentive or the threat of a penalty might be enough to get them to overcome the issue. However, it's often easier to fix the issue and eliminate the problem altogether.

LAYER #6: SUPPORT (THE HELP AND COACHING THAT STUDENTS NEED)

As far back as the 1980s, educational psychologist Benjamin Bloom and his team set out to measure the impact of mastery-based learning (meaning that students wouldn't progress to new material until they mastered the old material) and one-on-one tutoring on student achievement. He compared a regular classroom as the control with a lecture-based classroom that followed a mastery learning approach as variation A and a classroom with a mastery learning approach and one-on-one tutoring for students as variation B. The results were staggering: Variation A performed one standard deviation above the control, and variation B performed two standard deviations above the control.

In Bloom's words, "the average tutored student was above 98 percent of the students in the control class." This was a true breakthrough: a way of supporting 98 percent of the students to perform substantially above the current average. The challenge, of course, is the lack of money and teachers to provide one-on-one tutoring to every student. Statisticians use the Greek letter sigma to represent standard deviations, which led to the naming of Bloom's 2 Sigma

Problem: "to find a method of group instruction as effective as one-to-one tutoring."

Now, finally, we have the tools and resources to put Bloom's findings into practice, through an intelligent integration and hand-off between technology and human support. First comes mastery-based instruction, which means the student doesn't progress to lesson two until they've understood lesson one. The first step is to check on the comprehension and performance of a student and offer corrective feedback. This can be done not only by technology but also by peers. As Coursera co-founder Daphne Koller explains in her excellent TED talk, correctly structured and administered peer feedback structures yield the same returns to students as feedback from the teacher. And in my own experience implementing these same structures in a number of online courses, the best part is that students tend to learn the most from the process of providing feedback to their peers. When the peer feedback isn't enough, or a persistent issue arises, the feedback can be escalated to the support of a tutor or coach. The key isn't to avoid human support, but rather to apply it where it has the potential for the greatest leverage and impact.

ITERATE TO MAKE IT GREAT

If you've been around academia at some point in your career, you may have heard an old saying that's common in universities: You're just not comfortable in the classroom until you've taught a course for the third time. What this points to is that course design is a fundamentally iterative process. The first offering is full of questions and uncertainty, the second is much improved but also shows just how much more you could be doing, and the third delivers an excellent experience—but you're never really finished improving!

Here's how this generally plays out: You launch your pilot. It's time to work with your first cohort of students, and invariably you learn that your explanations aren't as clear as you thought, and your students aren't nearly as motivated as you expected. That's not to mention that your technology is hard to use, your accountability measures are proving ineffective, and the success behaviors that you painstakingly designed don't seem to be taking hold. Thankfully, you overcompensated with support for your students, and with what feels like Herculean effort, you get them over the finish line.

Then it's time to iterate and improve. Just as a book can and should undergo multiple rounds of revision, most courses must undergo multiple rounds of iteration. You develop the course, present it to students, and measure the results. This leads to learning about what worked and what didn't, plus hypotheses about how you might do better. That in turn leads to a new iteration, new feedback, and new learning, in a cycle that keeps on going. Student results improve over time, and you start seeing diminishing returns on new iterations and improvements. Your course is now robust. At long last, you've built something stable and truly transformative.

IF IT SCARES YOU...

*"Education is the most powerful weapon
which you can use to change the world."*
-NELSON MANDELA

ONLINE COURSES HAVE CHANGED MY LIFE.

As a student and learner, they've expanded my horizons and empowered me with valuable and meaningful skills; I've built important things in my business and life thanks to the things I've learned through online courses. And as a teacher and entrepreneur, I have been able to reach and serve more people than I ever would have imagined; my income has multiplied, and I have the leverage to make my wife and children the number one priority that they deserve to be.

I've shared different parts of this story over the years with the coaches, consultants, authors, speakers, and experts that I train. They see the opportunity that online courses creates for them to create this sort of leverage, freedom, and impact in their own businesses and lives. And when I speak with them, I always try to strike a balance between two very different tones.

On the one hand, there's the pep talk: "Look at this incredible opportunity that's just waiting to be seized"; "imagine the leverage you could create, the freedom you could experience, and the impact that you could make"; and "it worked for me and for all these people, so why wouldn't it work for you too?" These are fair statements to make, things my experience has led me to truly believe. At the same time, there are also the disclaimers—not the legal-type disclaimers of "I can't guarantee that you will be successful" (though, of course, I can't), but more about the things that I actually can guarantee: creating an online course business will take time, and energy, and focus. There will be challenges and setbacks along the way. Not everything you try will work.

Setting out on the path to support, augment, or transform your business with online courses is a bit like choosing to run a marathon. As long as you have the basic prerequisites in place (a base level of fitness for the marathon, and meaningful expertise in your field for online courses), it's not that hard. That is, if you're geared up for it—giving yourself the runway to train, fully prepared that some parts of the process will challenge you. Put another way, they're very attainable goals—so long as you take them seriously and don't expect to do them on a lark.

Online courses are one of the key levers that will up-level our society in the coming decades, and in the process they will create a great deal of prosperity for committed creators. Building yours is a worthy and exhilarating undertaking—and one that might give you a moment of trepidation. "Am I really doing this? Am I really ready? Do I want it enough?"

I love questions like these, because they show an expert who is taking the opportunity as seriously as it deserves. So I'll end by quoting Seth Godin: "If it scares you, it might be a good thing to try."

ADDITIONAL RESOURCES TO SUPPORT YOU!

GET THE AUDIOBOOK + COURSE BUSINESS TOOL KIT

Receive the free audiobook PLUS our Course Business Tool Kit, which contains valuable downloads and worksheets to help you create your own online course business.

→ Download it at **TeachYour.Gift/toolkit**

PARTICIPATE IN THE COURSE BUILDER'S BOOTCAMP

Ready to start your own online course business journey? Our weeklong intensive Course Builder's Bootcamp is a crash course in everything you need to get started.

→ Sign up for free at **TeachYour.Gift/bootcamp**

JOIN US IN PERSON AT TEACH YOUR GIFT LIVE

Receive best-in-class training, discover cutting-edge strategies, and connect with a community of your fellow coach, consultant, author, speaker, and expert course entrepreneurs.

→ Reserve your spot at **TeachYour.Gift/live**

DOWNLOAD THE AUDIOBOOK + COURSE BUSINESS TOOL KIT (FOR FREE)!

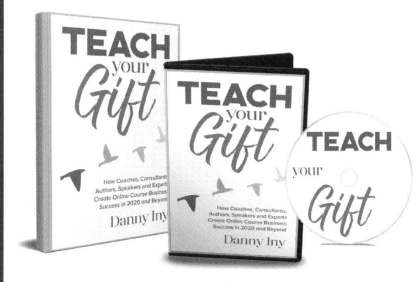

READ THIS FIRST

Just to say thank you for reading my book, I'd love to share the audiobook version PLUS our accompanying Course Business Tool Kit, at no cost whatsoever—it's my gift to you. — Danny Iny

Go to **TeachYour.Gift/toolkit** to get it!

MASSIVE GRATITUDE

IT IS CUSTOMARY TO INCLUDE a section at the end of the book where you acknowledge everyone who supported you along the way—but really, they deserve so much more than mere acknowledgement. What they really deserve is my massive gratitude, because this book (and all of my work) wouldn't be possible without them.

Topping the list are the wonderful people that I get to work with every day at Mirasee, where we teach coaches, consultants, authors, speakers, and experts to teach their gift and grow their businesses— and of course the students that we have the privilege of working with, supporting, and also learning from. And special thanks go to Abe Crystal, CEO of Ruzuku, my close friend, colleague, and collaborator in developing some of the key ideas shared in these pages.

Also deserving of appreciation are the entire Writer's Ally team that helped shepherd this book to publication; Allyson Machate, Sherrie Clark, Cecille Garcia, and Emily Hitchcock—thank you!

And most of all, my family. Bhoomi, you are my partner at home, and my partner at work. I hit the marriage jackpot, and I hope I never forget that. Priya and Micah, I'm so proud of how you're growing, and how much I learn every day from each of you.

ABOUT THE AUTHOR

DANNY INY is the founder and CEO of the online business education company Mirasee, whose work on strategy training won special recognition from *Fast Company* as a "World Changing Idea." He has been featured in the *Harvard Business Review* and *Entrepreneur*, and contributes regularly to publications including *Inc.*, *Forbes*, and *Business Insider.* He has spoken at institutions like Yale University and organizations like Google, and is the author of multiple books about online courses and education, including two editions of *Teach and Grow Rich* (in 2015 and 2017), and *Leveraged Learning* (in 2018). He lives in Montreal, Canada, with his wife Bhoomi (who is his partner in both life and business) and their children Priya and Micah.

Made in the USA
Columbia, SC
06 June 2020